D1544541

The Sound and the Fury
Faulkner and the Lost Cause

Twayne's Masterwork Studies

Robert Lecker, General Editor

The Sound and the Fury
Faulkner and the Lost Cause

John T. Matthews

Twayne Publishers * Boston
A Division of G. K. Hall & Co.

The Sound and the Fury: Faulkner and the Lost Cause
John T. Matthews

Copyright 1991 by G. K. Hall & Co.
All rights reserved.
Published by Twayne Publishers
A division of G. K. Hall & Co.
70 Lincoln Street
Boston, Massachusetts 02111

Copyediting supervised by Barbara Sutton.
Book production by Gabrielle B. McDonald.
Typeset in 10/14 Sabon
by Compset, Inc., of Beverly, Massachusetts.

First published 1990.
10 9 8 7 6 5 4 3 2 1 (hc)
10 9 8 7 6 5 4 3 2 1 (pb)

Library of Congress Cataloging-in-Publication Data

Matthews, John T.
The sound and the fury : Faulkner and the lost cause / John T.
Matthews.
p.   cm.—(Twayne's masterwork studies ; no. 61)
Includes bibliographical references and index.
ISBN 0-8057-7965-5 (alk. paper).—ISBN 0-8057-8018-1 (pbk. :
alk. paper)
1. Faulkner, William, 1897–1962.   Sound and the fury.   I. Title.
II. Series.
PS3511.A86S840   1990
813'.52—dc20   90-43006
                                         CIP

For My Parents

Contents

A Note on the References and Acknowledgments

The Sound and the Fury: The Corrected Text, edited by Noel Polk (New York: Random House, 1984; Vintage paperback, 1987) is the current standard text. Since virtually all students will be reading the paperback edition, I have quoted from this volume. Page citations follow quotations in parentheses. Two important supplementary documents, an introduction (in two versions) Faulkner wrote for a later edition of *The Sound and the Fury* and the so-called Compson Appendix (a key to the Compsons written by Faulkner in 1945), have been reprinted in the Norton Critical Edition of the novel edited by David L. Minter. I have restricted my references to material in this edition (abbreviated as NCE in the text), but students should know that the Norton Critical Edition reprints (with different pagination) the corrected text of the novel.

More than most kinds of writing about literature, a volume like this one—devoted to background and an introductory interpretation of a work of art—relies on the work of many other scholars. I have tried to indicate specific debts clearly and to guide readers to the abundance of interesting specialized work on Faulkner. I gratefully acknowledge those who have made me a better student of Faulkner by personally sharing their knowledge with me, many of them generously reading and commenting on portions of this manuscript: André Bleikasten, James Carothers, William Carroll, Richard Godden, Michel Gresset, James Hinkle, Laurence Holland, John Irwin, Arthur Kinney, Thomas McHaney, Susan Mizruchi, Richard Moreland, Patrick

A Note on the References and Acknowledgments

O'Donnell, Noel Polk, Stephen Ross, Warwick Wadlington, and Philip Weinstein. I thank Matthew L. Pelikan for his thorough, intelligent work as a research assistant on this project. Robert Lecker has been an unusually perceptive and patient editor.

Writing this book for students has happily coincided with our children's discovery of the pleasures of learning; so Lauren and Jamie have sometimes let me write when I might have been playing, though not so often as would have been bad for us. My wife, Sharon, has always given my work far more than it could hope to vindicate; I am grateful for her encouragement all the more. I am pleased to dedicate this book to my parents, Jack and Elva Matthews, who first helped me discover the gratifications of being a lifelong student.

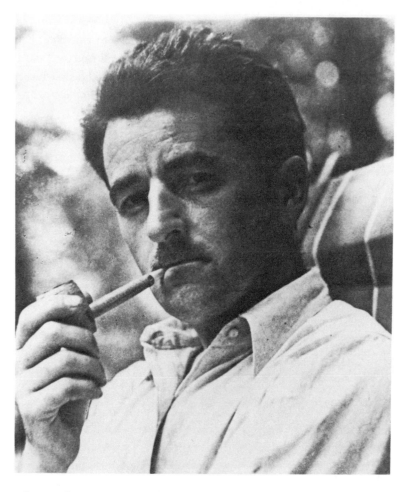

William Faulkner in August 1931, not quite two years after The Sound and the Fury *was published.*

Chronology: William Faulkner's Life and Works

1897   William Cuthbert Falkner, the first of four sons, is born 25 September to Murry C. and Maud Butler Falkner in New Albany, Mississippi. Murry Falkner (as the name was spelled before William added the "u" as a young man) was an administrator for the railroad built by his grandfather, the locally legendary William Clark Falkner (known to all as the "Old Colonel").

1914   Develops a friendship with his Oxford townsman Phil Stone (the Falkners had moved from New Albany to Ripley and finally to Oxford all before William was five years old). Deeply interested in modern literature and having studied at Yale, Stone suggests the directions of Falkner's early reading—Swinburne, Keats, Conrad, Aiken and Sherwood Anderson, among others. Four years older than Falkner, Stone becomes a lifelong friend (though with distinct periods of cooling later) and later helps Falkner publish his first work, a collection of poems.

1916–1917   Is involved with student publications at the University of Mississippi, whose campus is in Oxford. Publication of drawings and verse translations in *Ole Miss*, the student annual.

1918   After America joins World War I in 1917, attempts to enlist in the U.S. air corps but is rejected because he is too short. Eventually he is taken by the Royal Air Force of Canada, and he enters training in July 1918 in Toronto. The armistice of November sends him (now spelling his surname as he would for the rest of his life) back to Oxford before he can see any combat. For some time he is fond of telling stories about his war "injuries" and exploits, but eventually he admits these are tall tales.

1924   Continues to contribute his novice work to University of Mississippi student publications. He is also involved with the

University dramatic club (though he is never more than a part-time student), and writes a play entitled *Marionettes* for the group. Eventually a collection of poems is accepted for publication by the Four Seas Company in Boston; Phil Stone oversees the arrangements.

1925   *The Marble Faun,* a book of poems.

1925   Makes trip to New Orleans, where he involves himself with a circle of writers associated with the avant-garde literary magazine *The Double Dealer.* Publishes poems and short prose pieces in its pages. *The Double Dealer* also published early work by Hart Crane, Ernest Hemingway, Robert Penn Warren, and Edmund Wilson. Completes the typescript of *Soldiers' Pay,* his first novel. Horace Liveright, the New York publisher of Sherwood Anderson, accepts it, in part on the recommendation of Anderson. In July, with his friend artist William Spratling, sails for Genoa, Italy, from New Orleans. Working intermittently on both prose and poetry, travels through Italy, spends several months living in Paris, and returns to Mississippi by Christmas.

1927   Second novel, *Mosquitoes,* published by Liveright.

1928   Is completing a third book, *Flags in the Dust,* that inaugurates his fictional county, Yoknapatawpha. Liveright's rejection of the manuscript eventually leads him to place it with Harcourt, Brace, under the provision that it be cut substantially. Begins to write *The Sound and the Fury* in the spring and finishes by early fall. Meanwhile, his friend Ben Wasson, an editor for Harcourt, Brace, trims the manuscript of *Flags in the Dust.*

1929   *Sartoris,* the new title for the revised *Flags in the Dust,* is published by Harcourt, Brace. Is at work on his next novel, *Sanctuary.* *The Sound and the Fury* is rejected by Harcourt, Brace but accepted by a new publishing firm, Cape & Smith, one of whose partners, Harrison Smith, had been an enthusiastic editor of Faulkner's at Harcourt, Brace. Marries Estelle Oldham Franklin in June after her divorce became final in April. *The Sound and the Fury* published by Jonathan Cape and Harrison Smith on 7 October in an edition of 1,789 copies. The Faulkners' first child, Alabama, is born prematurely and dies after only a few days.

1930   *As I Lay Dying* published by Cape and Smith.

1931   *Sanctuary,* a novel composed before *As I Lay Dying* and later heavily revised, published.

1932   Accepts his first contract as a scriptwriter in Hollywood with

Metro-Goldwyn-Mayer at five hundred dollars per week. Murry Falkner, William's father, dies and Faulkner returns to Oxford from Hollywood. *Light in August* published by the new firm Harrison Smith and Robert Haas.

1933   The Faulkners' daughter Jill is born. Editor Bennett Cerf corresponds with Faulkner about a special reissue of *The Sound and the Fury* that would follow the author's suggestion that passages be printed in different color ink to indicate various time periods. Faulkner writes the drafts of an introduction for this edition and marks a copy of the novel to instruct printers about the color key. The project collapses, however, in part because of the country's generally worsened economic conditions. Faulkner's marked copy of the novel is now lost.

1934–1935   Is working on the manuscript of *Absalom, Absalom!* in Hollywood, where he again holds a scriptwriting contract. He returns to Oxford, interrupts *Absalom* to write *Pylon*, then takes up the Sutpen/Compson novel again. The second half of the book is written just after an air crash claims the life of Faulkner's youngest brother Dean, a professional pilot first encouraged to fly by Faulkner, himself an amateur aviator.

1936   *Absalom, Absalom!* published by Random House, which becomes Faulkner's permanent publisher.

1939   Elected to the National Institute of Arts and Letters.

1942   *Go Down, Moses and Other Stories*—a novel reworked from several earlier short stories that appeared during a span of about ten years, from the mid-thirties to the mid-forties, in which Faulkner's financial situation is nearly desperate. He continues to compose and market short stories for quick returns and accepts an unusually long but low-paying contract for scriptwriting from Warner Brothers.

1946   *The Portable Faulkner*, an anthology of short stories and excerpts from his novels, edited by Malcolm Cowley, who had first approached Faulkner about the idea. This volume contains the first printing of the so-called Compson Appendix, which chronicles the history of the family both up to and after the time of *The Sound and the Fury*.

1948   *Intruder in the Dust*. Its overt interest in the question of southern racial desegregation signals Faulkner's newfound willingness to address social issues. He writes a series of letters and public statements on racial problems in the South throughout the fifties.

1950   *Collected Stories*. Announcement that Faulkner has won the

1949 Nobel Prize for literature (as a corecipient with Bertrand Russell). On 10 December Faulkner delivers his acceptance speech to the Swedish Academy. His daughter, Jill, accompanies him to Stockholm.

1951   *Collected Stories* wins the National Book Award. Public recognition and the attendant popularity of his work assure Faulkner's financial security for the first time in his career. From this point until the end of his life becomes increasingly a public figure, accepting requests from the State Department to travel abroad to solidify cultural relations with allies and speaking out on several public issues, such as the cold war and desegregation.

1957   Is writer-in-residence at the University of Virginia. *The Town*, the second volume of the Snopes trilogy, published.

1959   *The Mansion*, the final volume of the trilogy, published.

1960   His mother, Maud Butler Falkner, dies in Oxford at the age of eighty-eight.

1962   On 6 July Faulkner dies unexpectedly of a probable heart attack in a clinic in Byhalia, Mississippi, after being hospitalized for several days following a horseback riding accident. His funeral takes place the next day in Oxford.

LITERARY AND HISTORICAL CONTEXT

1

frames of reference

Many Americans enjoyed unprecedented peace and prosperity during the 1920s. On 2 July 1921 the United States had ended its involvement in World War I in a treaty with the defeated Germany. Although the war's conclusion never realized President Woodrow Wilson's vision of world peace through international cooperation, it did allow U.S. banking and industry to consolidate and accelerate the success they had had in equipping and financing the Allied war effort.

Elected in 1912 as the first modern southern President, Wilson had led the country from its near consensus in support of neutrality (which he shared), to the eventual declaration of war in 1917. Wilson's ambitious design for international peace once the hostilities had been decided in favor of the Allies depended on forgoing harsh punishment of Germany and founding an organization to arbitrate international disputes, the League of Nations. Yet the Democratic president could not overcome largely Republican resistance in Congress, nor, nearly incapacitated by a stroke in 1919, could he mobilize public support for his plan. Warren G. Harding, the Republican candidate for president in 1920, considered his decisive victory a repudiation of the Treaty of Versailles and the League of Nations, one of the treaty's provisions.

In part the treaty's defeat must be attributed to nationalistic sentiments aroused by the war and confirmed by the economic advantages America enjoyed over war-weakened Europe. Although postwar prosperity wobbled briefly during the depression of 1921–22, Harding's laissez-faire posture successfully allowed business and industry to strengthen themselves as they saw fit. Harding's administration did extend some of the progressive measures advocated by labor and farm reformers during Wilson's tenure, but the Republican twenties mainly created a much warmer environment for business and financial interests. After Harding's death in office in 1923, a number of scandals—including the infamous Teapot Dome scandal—were exposed; yet his successor, Calvin Coolidge, who was eventually elected president in his own right in 1924, continued the legacy that "the business of America is business."

American industry had developed rapidly because of demands of the war. Industries like textiles and plastics flourished; building enjoyed a boom; and energy sources such as steam turbines and hydroelectric plants pushed ahead American productivity. Such changes in the material realities of the twenties transformed the lives of many people. The expansion of electrical service and the mass production of appliances, for example, remade the American home. Automobiles became cheap and plentiful—by 1925 a Model T Ford cost only $290, and by 1929 one in every five Americans owned a car. The country was being paved at a cost of one billion dollars per year. Air travel and radio contributed to the "shrinking" of the country and strengthened its sense of national identity.

One cost of American prosperity in the twenties was in the corresponding hostility to anything perceived as "un-American." The economic allure of the United States attracted thousands of immigrants from war-devastated Europe. Their arrival provoked harsh responses from those threatened by the impact of so many workers on the job market. Congress passed several quota acts during the early 1920s to restrict immigration. A more violent protest arose in the revival of the Ku Klux Klan in 1915 (the movement had originated in 1866 and expired after southern Reconstruction); the modern Ku Klux Klan took aim not only at blacks but also at Catholics, Jews, and foreigners for their alleged erosion of American morality and religion. Even the federal amendment against the sale of alcohol—the so-called Prohibition, a doomed experiment spanning the decade (1920–32)—espoused the cause of national purity.

The zealotry of such behavior suggests anxieties deeper than concerns about economic competition; Western civilization itself seemed at risk. Worshiping the cult of material prosperity, perhaps many Americans hoped to shake the disillusionment that followed the war. Not only was World War I astonishingly savage (the technology of combat "advanced" unprecedentedly to the machine gun, gas warfare and aerial combat), but it also dashed nineteenth-century confidence in social progress. Never before had war been conducted on such a scale; and never before had the suffering of soldiers and civilians been so immediately and graphically portrayed to homefront populations, who were consuming wired news accounts and photographs. Violence seemed a global achievement for the first time in history; and not a few witnesses wondered with T. S. Eliot's poetic persona Gerontion, "after such knowledge, what forgiveness?"

Countering those who stood behind the moral and economic "righteousness" that defended the American way from immigrants, unions, communists, blacks (the underclass, in a word), other segments of society chose to protest against these values. The celebrants of the so-called jazz age, though certainly dependent on their largely privileged status, nevertheless sought to flout the moral and social codes they associated with a repressive and superficial bourgeois mentality. Caddy Compson's audacious independence and open sexual behavior reflect this shift in moral standards among the young. F. Scott Fitzgerald's early novels have become hallmarks of this period; *This Side of Paradise* (1920) and *The Beautiful and Damned* (1922) swirl with the intoxicants of bootleg alcohol, witty repartee, scandalous sexual freedom, and a jaded appetite for novelty. The protagonist of the earlier novel, Amory Blaine, struggles to renew his hope during a season of postwar disillusionment amid "a new generation dedicated more than the last to the fear of poverty and the worship of success;

grown up to find all Gods dead, all wars fought, all faiths in man shaken" ([New York: Scribners, 1920, 1948], 282).

Though the celebrated flapper became the jazz age icon of the newly liberated woman, women made few serious gains during the decade. The Nineteenth Amendment, passed by the House in 1918 but blocked in the Senate for a year by southerners, had provided the right to vote for women beginning in August 1920. Women may have behaved with less restraint during the twenties, but there was virtually no improvement in their economic, political, or social status. Only perhaps in their personal life did they realize some improvement; birth control methods, electrical appliances, processed foods, and relaxed divorce laws furthered women's control over their own lives. In *The Sound and the Fury* one of Miss Quentin's boyfriends finds a discarded condom container, and Caddy, divorced by Herbert Head, goes on to marry and part with at least one more husband according to the Compson Appendix.

The forces of modernization affected the South in ways that accorded with its distinct situation and history. After the Compromise of 1877 had essentially returned political control of southern states to state governments, thereby ending the period of federally mandated Reconstruction, the South began to revive its fundamental values. Naturally, the Civil War had permanently altered the foundation of both the southern economy and race relations, but the social and economic structures that organized the Old South displayed a remarkable ability to survive into the so-called New South. In the period between the Civil War and World War I, the planter class transformed itself into a still largely dominant class of landowners and merchants. We learn from later remarks by Faulkner on the characters of *The Sound and the Fury* that Jason, for example, becomes the owner of a supply store in Jefferson, and thus demonstrates this conversion of the former planter class (in the generation of Jason's grandfather) into the new mercantile class.

Local economies remained tied to single crops, usually cotton. Blacks and poor whites continued to farm land belonging to others. The prevailing forms of agricultural relations were sharecropping, in which the laborer exchanged part of his crop for use of the land and the provision of equipment from the landowner, and share-renting, in which the renter paid a smaller proportion of his crop but had to furnish his own equipment. The crop-lien system deepened the rift between producers and sources of capital because storeowners would exchange goods and farm materials for a lien against the eventual crop.

The South's chronic undercapitalization blocked it from sharing equally in the prosperity of the rest of the country. In addition to these conditions in agriculture, southern industry, though it developed markedly after the Civil War, depended excessively on northern investment and management. While the rest of the nation flourished, the South once again seemed fated to failure. The national per capita income in 1900 was $1,165, but in the South it was $509. Paradoxically, some nationally beneficial advances actually deprived the South of sources of revenue; for example, the commercial and passenger trade on the Mississippi River vanished by the 1880s once railroads had spanned the country. Southerners felt these paradoxes acutely. On the one hand, they were enticed into cooperation with Yankee investment power and business methods; on the other, they realized that such modernization would destroy the very ideal of the South they cherished. Faulkner's own family was a legendary embodiment of these contradictions. His great-grandfather, William Clark Falkner (as the name was spelled originally), was a certified Confederate war hero and author of historical romances nostalgic of the Old South; yet he later helped found the Ripley Railroad Company and imagined the day when his corner of the Mississippi would be linked to the Chicago–New Orleans rail commerce.

From the end of radical Republican rule during Reconstruction in 1877 to the beginning of World War I, the South moved ambivalently and unevenly toward modernization. Many of the factors shaping pre–Civil War life in the South were immune to change: the region continued to rely mainly on cotton; far fewer immigrants to the South meant that class and economic categories lacked the fluidity of northern counterparts; and the nation's black population continued to live overwhelmingly in the South (still about 90 percent in 1900), confined, with poor white farmers, to dependence on the small class of landowners and merchants. Although lumbering and textiles led the growth of industry in the South, inspired by both southern entrepreneurs and transplanted Yankees looking for economic opportunity, the South lagged far behind the North's much more rapid industrialization. (By 1900 the South had only ten percent of the nation's factories—a smaller proportion than it had had in 1860.)

Politically, a governing class known as the Bourbons emerged after radical Republican rule. Gradually these Democrats, who called themselves the Redeemers in honor of their supposed salvation of the South from Reconstruction Republicanism, fostered business and industrial development and greatly reduced public spending in order to melt debt. Though they preserved some of the political gains made by blacks during Reconstruction, the Bourbons' main motives for keeping blacks enfranchised and in (at least lower level) political office involved their efforts to use black ballotry against poor white farmers' interests.

Eventually, black enfranchisement was sacrificed by the Democrats as they attempted to fend off Populism's amalgamation of poor black and white farmers. The sharp depression of the political status of blacks beginning in the 1890s and lasting well into the 1960s coincided with the general degeneration of racial relations in the South. Civil rights for blacks also deteriorated under state laws that created a "Jim Crow" society, one in which "separate but equal" became official doctrine even as it was being used to justify outrageous inequities. By 1910, the earliest date of narration in *The Sound and the Fury*, blacks had begun organizing protest groups, including the National Association for the Advancement of Colored People (NAACP), which grew out of a conference held on Lincoln's birthday in 1909.

•　　•　　•

Descending from a legendary southern patriarch like his great-grandfather, the "Old Colonel," William Faulkner's earliest memories must have included stories about the Old South Falkners, particularly those told by his cherished Aunt Alabama. Those stories certainly included mythic elements: the young William Falkner's setting off as a foundling from Missouri in search of a prosperous uncle in Mississippi and finding him in Pontotoc in 1840; his success in reading law in his uncle's office and rising to become a prominent plantation master (and slave owner); his Civil War fame, celebrated by General Beauregard's certificate of valor proclaiming that history would forever remember his exploits; his return to Ripley and political and entrepreneurial dominance. The Old Colonel passed his mantle to his son, John Wesley Thompson Falkner (1848–1922), who continued the family's ambitiousness by practicing law, managing political campaigns, running his father's railroad, and founding Oxford's first bank.

Yet the family history also carried less proud moments: the Old Colonel's extraordinary affinity for violence, which culminated in his assassination at the hands of a former business partner; his armed opposition to black voter registration during Reconstruction; the so-called Young Colonel's sale of the railroad that his son would have inherited, and the eventual decay of the Falkner family fortune under the ineptness and despair of that offspring, Murry Falkner, the novelist's father.

Murry was a silent, unhappy man, apparently unfit for the responsibilities into which he was born. His professional life was comprised of a series of failed opportunities; he finally finished his career as assistant secretary of the University of Mississippi, a job he got, like many others, through family connections. As Murry might have, Jason Compson, whose voice Murry's closely resembled according to the author's mother, both rages at the loss of a better world in the idealized Old South and accepts its passing because it has done no good for him.

Murry's oldest son proved capable of repeating similar sentiments about the destruction of the Old South. In an introduction written (but not published at the time) for a planned reissue of *The Sound and the Fury* in 1933, Faulkner complains that "[t]here is a thing known whimsically as the New South to be sure, but it is not the South. It is a land of Immigrants who are rebuilding the towns and cities into replicas of towns and cities in Kansas and Iowa and Illinois . . . and teaching the young men who sell the gasoline and the waitresses in the restaurants to say O yeah? and to speak with hard r's" ("An Introduction," *Mississippi Quarterly*, 411; NCE, 221). In part Faulkner shares Quentin's and Jason's recoil from the modernized South, the land of foreigners, Yankees, and impersonal monetary relations. *The Sound and the Fury* surely registers a variety of resistances to the breakup of the Old South's mentality. Yet Faulkner's fiction—beginning with tendencies we will discuss in *The Sound and the Fury*—also considers how the myths of the Old South masked and rationalized repugnant social practices.

Faulkner's attitude toward the complex history and tradition into which he was born remained contradictory. A piece of family legend recounts how, when asked by a grade school teacher what he wanted to be when he grew up, Billy Falkner replied that he wanted to be a writer, just like his great-granddaddy. Yet the Old Colonel was not only an author, of course; he was, as we have seen, an active designer of the Old South as well. Nor could his great-grandson's fiction end up celebrating the way of life his great-grandfather's romances honored; how many scenes in Faulkner's writing involve young men shocked by the revelation that the world they inhabit rests on racial, class, and gender oppression. Faulkner's writing is the very activity that forces him to confront the contradictions of his world.

The young William's early achievements owed much to his mother and her family, the Butlers. Maud Butler Falkner tempered her husband's harsh and often disapproving treatment of their four sons, especially their eldest, Bill. She was an amateur painter and encouraged her son's verbal and graphic abilities. Ambitious for all her sons, but particularly William, she recognized his native abilities early. Faulkner's school years began successfully, but by the middle elementary grades he had become a bored and largely indifferent student. Throughout his high school years Faulkner followed his artistic pursuits; he composed poems for friends, told legendary ghost stories to a Boy Scout troop he headed for a while, and generally behaved as a talented misfit in Oxford.

In Faulkner's later adolescence he developed a close, important friendship with a slightly older townsman, Phil Stone. Stone had been a law student at Yale and returned to Oxford full of passionate enthusiasms for modern literature. He told Faulkner what to read, and the two of them discussed their tastes and Faulkner's literary ambitions. Stone contributed to Faulkner's self-education and later helped to get Faulkner's first literary products published, a collection of poems. Stone reinforced Faulkner's interest in literary modernism—the poetry of T. S. Eliot, for example, and the French symbolist poets (such as Baudelaire and Verlaine). Like many cultivated young people, Faulkner and his acquaintances on the campus of the University of Mississippi followed developments in modern art and literature avidly (see Hönnighausen 1987). Faulkner published poems in the student newspaper and composed drawings for the annual yearbook; he also wrote a play, *Marionettes*, for the university drama club. These experimentations in modernist art forms, youthful as they were, eventually contributed to the modernist technique of *The Sound and the Fury*.

When World War I began abroad in 1914, the grandson of the Old Colonel began to dream of a new theater for heroic splendor. (Faulkner explores the relation between this modern war's appeal to southern youth and the Civil War's appeal to his great-grandfather's generation in *Sartoris*, his third novel.) Eventually Faulkner tried to enlist in the American armed forces for aviation training but was turned down because he was too short (Faulkner was five feet five and a half inches tall). He found his way to Toronto, where the Royal Air Force accepted him for flight training. Before he ever saw action in Europe, the war ended and Faulkner returned to Mississippi from Canada. For a while Faulkner drifted around Oxford, and finally ended up in New Orleans in late 1924.

These months in New Orleans were pivotal because they confirmed Faulkner in his literary ambitions. He was working on what would become his first published novel by this time; *Soldiers' Pay* (1926) described the painful and finally fatal return of a wounded war veteran to his small southern town (in Georgia). Faulkner had known the American writer Sherwood Anderson's fiancée during a brief stay in New York City, and when he arrived in New Orleans, where the Andersons lived, he was introduced to the writer he so respected. During the course of their early friendship, Anderson arranged to have his publisher look at Faulkner's manuscript. After its acceptance, Faulkner's vocation, if not his success, seemed assured, especially since the reviews of the novel were on the whole quite good.

Faulkner's second novel was called *Mosquitoes* (1927). In many ways uncharacteristic of later work, this was a novel of ideas. A diverse company of acquaintances join their hostess on a yachting party on the waters of Lake Pontchartrain near New Orleans. The party, including a number of artists, spends the time discussing the nature of art and its relation to other basic human drives, especially sexual desire. It is as if Faulkner paused for a highly self-conscious moment in this novel to examine the nature of his profession, and then chose next to write a massive book that surveys the fictional domain he would develop throughout the rest of his career.

Published as *Sartoris* in 1928, the novel that preceded *The Sound and the Fury* stakes out the region and characters that make up the so-called Yoknapatawpha county, Faulkner's fictional locale. Families like the Sartorises and Snopeses, who had figured in earlier unpublished manuscripts, here find coherent introduction. Faulkner begins to assess the economic, racial, and social components of northwest Mississippi, what he once called "his postage stamp of native soil" (*Lion*, 255).

Horace Liveright, publisher of Faulkner's first two novels, rejected the manuscript of this novel, then called *Flags in the Dust*, because it was "diffuse and nonintegral with neither very much plot development nor character development" (Blotner 1984, 205). Faulkner was stunned by this reaction, but held to his conviction that the novel was good: "I still believe it is the book which will make my name for me as a writer" (Blotner 1984, 206; *Selected Letters*, 39). He tried revising the novel but finally decided to put it away because he felt unable to make it shorter and simpler while preserving its integrity.

At this point Faulkner said he decided to "shut a door between me and all publishers' addresses and book lists. I said to myself, Now I can write" ("An Introduction," *Southern Review*, 710; NCE, 220). Faulkner's recollections of the intense privacy of making a book entirely for himself, with no idea that it would ever be read by anyone else, reinforce the legendary difficulty of *The Sound and the Fury*. Readers have often suspected that the novel makes no compromises with the reader because Faulkner never wanted to have any readers, but that seems demonstrably untrue judging from the enormous pride he took in his achievement. A friend and literary agent, Ben Wasson, had in fact managed to interest the publisher Alfred Harcourt in *Flags in the Dust*, and invited Faulkner to New York City to help cut the novel to Harcourt's specifications. Faulkner brought along the nearly finished manuscript of *The Sound and the Fury*, and, after putting the last touches on the book, tossed it toward Ben saying, "Read this, Bud. It's a real son-of-a-bitch" (Blotner 1984, 225). By all accounts Faulkner was fondest of this novel, his "heart's darling." A translator of his work into French reported that years after *The Sound and the Fury* had been published, Faulkner could recite page after page by heart. It is probably more helpful to think of Faulkner's attitude as one of having accepted the fact that his fiction could never reach a popular audience, and that his art would have to create its own readership over the course of time. This has been borne out. A number of discriminating readers and reviewers applauded Faulkner's early fiction, including *The Sound and the Fury*. But it was not until the early 1950s, long after Faulkner's major novels had been written, that his reputation as a classic writer was assured.

2

the importance of the work

The Sound and the Fury is one of those works whose greatness becomes ever after associated with its author's highest achievement. Anyone informed about the literary heritage of America today—more than a half a century after the novel's publication—thinks immediately of The Sound and the Fury at the mention of Faulkner's name. Like The Divine Comedy for Dante, Hamlet or King Lear for Shakespeare, Paradise Lost for Milton, Moby-Dick for Melville, or The Scarlet Letter for Hawthorne, The Sound and the Fury embodies for many readers the most representative attributes of Faulkner's subject and style.

At a crucial moment in Faulkner's personal and imaginative life, the composition of this novel taught him, as he himself said later, what it meant to write. By that Faulkner intended to distinguish the mere satisfactions of his earlier work from the "ecstasy" of writing The Sound and the Fury. In retrospect, we can see that Faulkner's fourth novel wed for the first time Faulkner's growing interest in his southern region's history with his continuing commitment to modernist aesthetics. In The Sound and the Fury one can appreciate the novelist's depiction of several representative southern mentalities, his indirect chronicling of a collapsing moral and social order through the portrayal of the decay of the Compson family, the representation of psychological states of mind through "stream-of-consciousness" technique, and his fragmentation of narrative line into nonchronological segments. This embodiment of so much that is Faulknerian is surely an important part of what we mean by calling *The Sound and the Fury* a "masterwork."

At the same time, works we consider consummate achievements often represent the fullest realization of trends in subject or technique that come to be seen as prevalent or characteristic after the fact—as we interpret the aesthetic history of the period in which they appear. *The Sound and the Fury* may strike us first as a remarkably bold and uncompromising technical experiment. Much of what first baffles us and then may seduce us about the novel involves its artistic stunts: describing the world from an idiot's point of view, or letting us overhear the deranged musings of a suicide's last hours, or forcing us to endure the scorching rage and contempt of a bigot like Jason. And the novel, after trying to render mentality from the inside out, then turns its technique around to try a more familiar objective description, from a third-person apparently omniscient point of view. Part of the enduring significance of *The Sound and the Fury* derives from Faulkner's achievement in breaking down and then reconstructing many of the conventions of realistic fiction. He makes us notice the instruments— the kinds of language, the varieties of points of view, the imposition of structure on time and mind—that in some kinds of realistic fiction become invisible because of the effort to sustain the illusion of presenting reality in its immediacy. From this vantage, *The Sound and the Fury* constitutes one of the fullest examples of the modernist novel in American literature.

Such technical innovativeness has a certain interest of its own, of course, but in the case of *The Sound and the Fury* Faulkner's technique empowers a strongly original treatment of his subject matter too. The general plot of the novel suggests a staple of American Gothic literature: the decline of the aristocratic family. Drawing on the conventions of a familial curse, overweening patriarchal pride, incestuous and narcissistic desire between members of the house, and a violent tension between the suppression and expression of passion, the Gothic novel—from its earliest instances in English at the end of the eighteenth century (*The Castle of Otranto* by Sir Hugh Walpole, for example)—has been concerned with social decay and transition. It is no accident, as Leslie Fiedler argues in *Love and Death in the American Novel* (1975), that the Gothic should be a very important strain in American fiction, for the Gothic's concentration on psychological questions and the internal dynamics of the family allow the American novelist material that would be unavailable to the novelist of manners. The alleged thinness of social life in America, its lack of institutions and a finely articulated life of customs, drove the writer of fiction in nineteenth-century America toward the romance, including the Gothic. Gothic fiction is the domain of the psychological novel in the nineteenth century. Nathaniel Hawthorne, for instance, makes use of Gothic conventions to explore the spiritual lives of the allegorical figures in much of his short fiction and in *The Scarlet Letter*, or to survey the decay across several generations of the Pyncheon family in *The House of the Seven Gables*. In *The Sound and the Fury* Faulkner brilliantly suggests this context even as he discards the outer mechanisms of the Gothic; the modernist form of the novel makes us confront the obsolescence of both an outmoded way of life and an outmoded habit of novelistic representation. Faulkner's modernism is as much a rebuff to nineteenth-century romances that celebrated antebellum life, to the Gothic preoccupation with psychological rather than historical fatedness (parodied in the psychological grotesques of *The Sound and the Fury*), and to the specific legacies of the Old South as it is a fashionable embrace of international aesthetic modernism.

The Sound and the Fury constitutes what most critics have recognized as Faulkner's "breakthrough to mastery" (Bleikasten 1982, xi). As such, it certainly displays the author's technical virtuosity in the first flower of its full maturity. But *The Sound and the Fury*'s power also is generated by the very personal nature of its thematic material. Connections between a work and its author's inner life always remain complicated: How can we get access to these states of mind except through the literary texts or other texts like letters or interviews? How do we know whether the inner life creates the conditions for the writing, or whether the needs of the writer may not create a theater for psychic activity as an aftereffect of the writing? Nevertheless, the facts of Faulkner's life and times make it clear that he might have had reasons for expressing the profound nostalgia and sense of loss that prevail in the novel.

We will see that *The Sound and the Fury* addresses conflicts between the sense of lost innocence and the need to mature, between the privacy of grief and the urge to express sorrow, between the dream of the South's moral and spiritual ideals and the actuality of its history. Faulkner referred to some intensely intimate problems he was suffering at the time of the novel's composition; and at least one source of the work's preoccupations must have been his expected marriage to Estelle Oldham Franklin, the woman he had loved virtually from childhood who was in the last stage of a divorce from her first husband. Faulkner must have thought deeply about what it meant to have lost that innocent love only to be on the threshold of regaining it on the other side of "purity." This consideration of loss and desire may have been reinforced by Faulkner's ruminations on the scenes of his own childhood—his intimate play with his two middle brothers and their cousin, Sallie Murry Wilkins. All the Faulkner brothers recall the trauma of their grandmother's death and funeral, an event that took place in 1906; Faulkner was nine when his own "Damuddy" (the Faulkner grandchildren's nickname for their maternal grandmother) died.

The Sound and the Fury is not an autobiographical novel in the usual sense, and yet most readers sense the immediacy of its crises to the author. Part of the significance of the novel arises from its universalization of these common experiences. Moreover, these personal circumstances must have seemed all the more poignant against the background of the mighty social upheavals that seemed to be changing the face of the rural South. The changes in the Faulkner family's status and fortune, the rise of formerly dispossessed classes such as the poor white hill folk and blacks, meant that an old order was passing. The personal nature of the novel's subject matter may help to account for

Faulkner's own repeated preference for this novel: it was, he says, the one he felt most tender towards, "my heart's darling" (*University*, 6).

My subtitle, "Faulkner and the Lost Cause," is meant to suggest the several contexts for loss in *The Sound and the Fury*. "The Lost Cause" is a phrase that Southerners made popular after the Civil War as they struggled to absorb the reality of defeat in the face of continued belief in the righteousness of their cause. The myth of the Lost Cause flourished in the 1880s and 1890s when the South hoped to erase the humiliation of northern occupation during the Reconstruction period (ending officially in 1877). Southerners began to pay more open tributes to the Confederacy's fallen but unbowed heroes. The New South appeared to rise from the ruins of the Old South, needing both to recognize the loss of an irrecoverable way of life but also to imagine restoring its essence under altered circumstances. These contradictory attitudes were partially held together by ideas like the Lost Cause, which allowed its adherents to accept defeat without surrendering faith. As one Civil War veteran puts it in another of Faulkner's novels, "Well, Kernel, they mought have whupped us but they aint kilt us yit, air they?" (*Absalom*, 349). The South's preoccupation with mourning the past is captured in the Compson brothers' attitudes toward the "lost" Caddy, whose recovery becomes the doomed cause of the Compson family. Faulkner investigates the highly individual mentalities of his characters, yet the personal eccentricities of the Compsons also turn out to reveal much about the mentality of the South in the period between the 1890s and 1920s.

Faulkner's many paradoxical formulations of the problems of loss and desire in the novel lead to an extraordinarily complex and demanding work of art. The many difficulties for the reader of *The Sound and the Fury* make up part of the popular image of the novel. How many students (and even professional critics) have confessed to bafflement in their efforts to interpret the novel. Respecting the sheer difficulty of deciphering the sentences on the page in any first reading of *The Sound and the Fury*, I have organized this book according to several well-recognized approaches to the novel's meaning. The next section tells the story of the composition and publication of *The*

Sound and the Fury, sketching the conditions in the novelist's literary and social spheres, the circumstances of his life, and the work's critical reception. In subsequent chapters I consider main elements of the work: its characters, technique, and setting.

Among my purposes in this volume, the most important is to convey to the beginning reader of Faulkner the very deep pleasures of comprehending a novel that has spoken and continues to speak profoundly to our culture. I hope to suggest how the difficulties of reading are themselves central to *The Sound and the Fury*'s meaning, and to stimulate the reader's further reflection (and rereading).

Like most acknowledged masterpieces, *The Sound and the Fury* has been the subject of a great deal of study. Thoughtful readers will want to consult some of this scholarship themselves, and another of my objectives here will be to indicate how they may pursue their interests in some of the topics raised by my interpretation. The resources for the study of Faulkner's work are rich; we have first-rate biographies, bibliographic listings of the scholarship, many important critical interpretations, and published facsimiles of Faulkner's manuscripts and typescripts. *The Sound and the Fury* has been newly edited (correcting errors in the original printed version). My remarks in what follows take this wealth of scholarship as their basis. I have cited specific indebtedness, but I leave it to the interested reader to follow out the ideas that have already been studied, and perhaps to see what might yet be discovered by fresh eyes.

3

composition and critical reception

One tendency in criticism of *The Sound and the Fury* has been reinforced by Faulkner's own view of the importance of this novel to his development as a writer. In the interviews and class conferences recorded during his residence at the University of Virginia (1957–58), Faulkner repeatedly referred to the novel as his favorite—often for the paradoxical reason that it was the one that "was the best failure": "It was the one that I anguished the most over, that I worked the hardest at, that even when I knew I couldn't bring it off, I still worked at it. It's like the parent feels toward the unfortunate child, maybe. The others that have been easier to write than that, and in ways are better books than that, but I don't have the feeling toward any of them that I do toward that one, because that was the most gallant, the most magnificent failure" (*University*, 61). In the introduction written for the intended 1933 reissue of the novel, Faulkner enlarges on what *The Sound and the Fury* meant to him:

> [W]hen I finished The Sound and The Fury I discovered that there is actually something to which the shabby term Art not only can, but must, be applied. I discovered then that I had gone through all

that I had ever read, from Henry James through Henty to newspaper murders, without making any distinction or digesting any of it, as a moth or a goat might. After The Sound and The Fury and without needing to open another book and in a series of delayed repercussions like summer thunder, I discovered the Flauberts and Dostoievskys and Conrads whose books I had read ten years ago. ("An Introduction," *Southern Review*, 708; NCE, 218)

Putting these comments side by side, we may see that Faulkner considered *The Sound and the Fury* the novel in which he broke through to maturity as a serious writer. It was the book, according to his view, through which he acquired the authority to join the ranks of James, Flaubert, Dostoyevsky, and Conrad, those important literary precursors who variously shaped the modern novelistic tradition to which Faulkner's own works were henceforth to belong.

Faulkner's confidence may surprise, but he was never falsely modest. Acquaintances even from his New Orleans days, when he was twenty-eight and had published scarcely a word anyone had read, recall how he sat with friends describing his ambitions, certain that he would eventually write works as memorable as Shakespeare's (no less). Faulkner's use of a phrase from Shakespeare's *Macbeth* as the title of his favorite novel may indicate his willingness to be measured against the highest standard. (Macbeth laments his wife's death with a soliloquy on her passing that refers to life as "a tale / Told by an idiot, full of sound and fury, / Signifying nothing" [5.5.27–28].) Also something of a sportsman, Faulkner was fond of saying that he was the kind of writer who kept one eye on the ball and one on Babe Ruth.

Part of the allure of *The Sound and the Fury* through the decades has been precisely its mythical status. Critics have imitated Faulkner's account of the novel because it comes closest to capturing the dream the author had for it; namely, it is a novel that succeeds paradoxically because it fails so spectacularly to express the ineffable vision of the beautiful innocence of childhood through the screen of adult alienation and loss. In this regard, Faulkner's description of the novel's genesis—the image of Caddy climbing the pear tree to look in at Damuddy's funeral while her brothers watch her muddy drawers disappear above them—reinforces the strain between the unutterable vision and the perishable breath (as F. Scott Fitzgerald put it in another spectacularly romantic novel of the same period, *The Great Gatsby*).

To his French translator in the mid-1930s Faulkner referred mysteriously to personal difficulties he was experiencing about the time he was writing the novel. In retrospect it seems clear that part of his emotional stake in "manufactur[ing]" the sister he never had and the daughter he would lose in infancy arises from the imminent prospect of recovering his childhood sweetheart, Estelle Oldham Franklin. With her two children, Estelle had left her husband, returned to Oxford (from the Orient), and clearly meant to resume her relationship with the ardent Bill Faulkner she had left behind. Faulkner at this point may have been far less sure about wanting to marry Estelle than when they had been high school and college sweethearts (her parents had forbidden their marriage initially because Faulkner seemed a ne'er-do-well). But Faulkner decided it was best that they marry, the ceremony taking place in June of 1929. *The Sound and the Fury* had been completed in the spring and summer of 1928 and accepted for publication the following spring, so throughout the period in which he was writing the novel, Faulkner was contemplating the recovery of the heart's darling of his youth. Surely his deep consideration of the relation between innocence and experience, between sexual "purity" and carnal knowledge, between the dreamt ideal and the possessed reality wells up in his personal emotional life during this time.

Likewise, though Faulkner emphasized the uniqueness of *The Sound and the Fury* both in his career and as an experimental novel, recent scholarship has uncovered plausible lines of development from Faulkner's apprentice writing and reading toward his breakthrough novel. In his poetry and prose sketches Faulkner experimented with lyrical effects that seemed to arrest time and lift the speaker out of history (indeed, his poems are often dreamy, narcissistic reveries that anticipate Quentin Compson's meditations on himself and his beloved). The fragmentary structure of the novel owes something to Faulkner's experiments with form in his poem cycle *Vision in Spring* (see Sensibar 1984). Some of the novel's mood and imagery descend from Faulkner's interest in the modern lyrics of T. S. Eliot, in whose depiction of postwar alienation and the paralysis of those still governed by Victorian codes of morality and heroism Faulkner found a deep resonance with his own situation. James Joyce's experiments with stream-of-consciousness style represented to Faulkner a way to create the immediacy of thought in the "slower" medium of language. Finally, Freud's powerful speculation about depth psychology opened the realms of the unconscious and preconscious to literary investigation and representation.

Yet Faulkner consistently denied many of these modern influences on his work, saying, for example, that he had never read either Freud or Joyce, but that friends in New Orleans had discussed their work and that he had learned of these authors in that way. (It turns out that Faulkner knew enough about Joyce firsthand to bring a copy of *Ulysses* along on his honeymoon in the summer of 1929 and to suggest that Estelle read it.) Faulkner seemed intent on mystifying the emergence of *The Sound and the Fury* in his creative life, as if he wished to give it a mythical aura. In a number of ways, the origin of *The Sound and the Fury* became obscured, as if it sprang without warning from Faulkner's personal life, writing career, aesthetic context, and regional vision—with no apparent connections to its history. As we will see, at least one of the reasons for the novel's tendency to be mythicized is its suppression of both historical material about the South and personal material about desire and identity that were too painful for Faulkner to confront directly at this point in his career.

The handwritten drafts (referred to as the holograph version by scholars) show that *The Sound and the Fury* was not an easy book to write. (See the facsimile holograph and the Morrison article in the *Casebook*.) Faulkner headed the first page with the title "Twilight" and composed a version of the Benjy section. The second part—Quentin's monologue—began with a scene between Caddy and Quentin at the branch after she has lost her virginity to Dalton Ames. Eventually, of course, Faulkner placed this scene later in the section, but its initial position suggests that it follows conceptually from the conclusion of Benjy's section, which also involves flashbacks to scenes of

Caddy's loss. Some of Faulkner's revisions actually loosen the structural continuity of the novel, then, as if he wishes to emphasize the disruptive form and style of his text.

This reduction of conventional unifying features explains a number of other revisions: the discarding of clarifying punctuation and quotation marks, the addition of several stream-of-consciousness passages, and the consistent but complicated use of italics to indicate time zones in Benjy's memory. On the other hand, Faulkner also added some thematic material in revision that elaborated on the characters' preoccupations, especially Quentin's. Added passages increase the presence of Mr. Compson as a character and heighten the sexual anxiety in Quentin's section. Such revisions show that Faulkner aimed at unifying his novel, but he wanted to do so through the radical experiment of eliminating narrative staples like authorial description and exposition. Instead, the unifying principles would emerge from the repetition of images, phrases, sensations.

Though the manuscript turns out to be remarkably close to the printed version, it was Faulkner's practice to type and revise his handwritten draft before submitting it to a publisher. This typescript is the version of the novel that he finished in Wasson's room in New York City, as I have previously mentioned, and which would have been used by the printers to set their type. Both the manuscript and typescript show that Faulkner reworked the novel's details considerably before he was satisfied with it.

One aspect of Faulkner's craft in *The Sound and the Fury* appears through the record of revision. As he composed, Faulkner took great care in the unorthodox punctuation and the spatial arrangement of passages on the page. At some stage of revision he removed quotation marks around dialogue from the manuscript. Likewise, the italicized portions of Benjy's section did not simply indicate the past as opposed to the present, which appeared in roman type. Rather, each shift in type was meant to convey a shift in time periods, of which at least a dozen are distinguishable in Benjy's memory. Faulkner was quite emphatic on this point. His friend Ben Wasson edited the typescript for the publishers, Jonathan Cape and Harrison Smith, then returned it to Faulkner with his editorial changes in preparation for publication. (This is a standard process called copyediting, in which the publisher's editorial staff checks for mechanical errors in grammar or spelling and makes suggestions for clarification.) Faulkner was shocked to see that Wasson had regularized the italicized sections (making everything either italicized type for past or roman type for present), had added a few clarifying phrases, and had changed punctuation. Faulkner responded sharply; after telling Wasson to restore his indications for type and punctuation, he also cautioned his friend not to tamper with his prose: "And dont make any more additions to the script, bud. I know you mean well, but so do I" (*Selected Letters*, 44–45).

The publishing firm Harcourt, Brace had rejected the manuscript of *The Sound and the Fury,* and so in all likelihood had Boni & Liveright (who still held an option on whatever novel Faulkner wrote after *Flags in the Dust,* which they had also rejected). It was not until Harrison Smith left Harcourt, Brace to form his own small company with Cape that the novel found a publisher. Having begun the novel in the spring of 1928, Faulkner finished his typescript revision in the fall. Nearly a year passed before the novel appeared, on 7 October 1929, in an edition of 1,789 copies. Smith believed firmly in Faulkner's talent and in the achievement of *The Sound and the Fury.* In tribute to its importance, as well as with respect to the difficulties he knew it would present even to sophisticated readers, Smith arranged for one of the firm's more popular serious writers, Evelyn Scott, to provide a brief appreciation of the novel to be included as a pamphlet with the first edition. Scott had read the novel in manuscript and liked it enormously; she volunteered her comments, and thus the critical reception of *The Sound and the Fury* began, somewhat oddly, at the very moment of its appearance.

Scott places the novel in the tragic tradition, suggesting that Faulkner gave "all the spacious proportions of Greek art" to his "story of the fall of a house, the collapse of a provincial aristocracy in a final debacle of insanity, recklessness, [and] psychological perversion" (Bassett 1975, 76–77). Scott appreciates the modernist technique of the novel; she mentions its resemblance, for example, to Joyce's experiments with "free association." She sees that the essential differences between the Compson brothers' personalities reflect different ways of responding to the loss of Caddy and the world she represents. Scott nicely balances the universal and local interests of Faulkner by noticing, on the one hand, how characters serve as universal types (Benjy as a Christ figure, Dilsey as the soul or conscience), and on the other hand, how the novel deals with "the new South" and cultural upheaval.

Other favorable reviews found the same virtues. Henry Nash Smith praised *The Sound and the Fury* for simultaneously reaching the level of universal tragedy in "the spectacle of a civilization uprooted and left to die" (Bassett 1975, 86) and also digging "minutely and understandingly [into] a given milieu and a given tradition." Faulkner's modernist technique—repeatedly noted as Joycean—won similar applause. Of course, even respectful reviewers admitted the sheer difficulty of the novel, and some predicted that the "public . . . will be indifferent or contemptuous or openly hostile" (Bassett 1975, 91), as indeed they were. But all in all *The Sound and the Fury* attracted admiring, intelligent reviews.

Throughout the 1930s scholarly critical opinion was divided on Faulkner's achievement. Detractors fell largely into two camps: those who objected to Faulkner's work on the ground that it was preoccupied with morbid, sensationalistic subject matter, and those who faulted him, along with other "high art" novelists, for failing to write politically engaged fiction during a period of strong activist commitment among writers. Both of these objections were aimed at Faulkner's subsequent novels—especially *Sanctuary* (1931)—as much as at *The Sound and the Fury*. *Sanctuary* told the story of the sexual assault of a Mississippi coed at the hands of an underworld thug who, impotent himself, violates her with a corncob and then arranges for her imprisonment in a Memphis brothel, where he spies on her lovemaking with the man to whom she is genuinely attracted. The novel's lurid, nightmarish scenes of violence and sex may be taken seriously as part of Faulkner's continuing meditation on the loss of personal and cultural innocence, but many critics found the novel was only an example of the degraded subgenre of "cult of cruelty" fiction. Because of its representation of Jason's vicious bigotries and violence, and in its parade of small-town grotesques—the idiots, suicides, "nymphomaniacs," hypochondriacs, and drunkards of Faulkner's declining Yoknapatawpha southern aristocracy—*The Sound and the Fury* suffered under simplistic denigration.

On the other hand, intelligent essays on the novel began to appear by the end of its first decade of publication. The French intellectual Jean-Paul Sartre wrote an extremely influential study of time in *The Sound and the Fury* (1939; translation, 1955). Though Sartre concentrates almost exclusively on Quentin's section and exaggerates the extent to which this one character speaks for the whole novel and so Faulkner, the essay brilliantly demonstrates how the past entirely overshadows the present in the novel. Sartre remarks the ubiquity of imagery referring to clocks, arguing that Quentin's obsession with what *was* destroys his present and "decapitates" his future. The past's destructiveness in Faulkner particularly impresses Sartre because at this point he was working through a contrasting philosophy of time; in *Nausea,* published about the same time as the essay on *The Sound and the Fury* (1939), Sartre presents a protagonist—named Roquentin—who discovers the powerful freedom of willing a future, of creating a self through an active reconsideration of his past.

Faulkner's astonishing achievements throughout the 1930s made it much easier for critics to appreciate the virtues of *The Sound and the Fury* in retrospect. After *As I Lay Dying* (1930), *Light in August* (1932), and *Absalom, Absalom!* (1936) had all made their mark as major novels (in a decade when Faulkner wrote a number of other fine novels as well), critics began to sketch the outlines of Faulkner's development, dating the beginning of his mature phase from *The Sound and the Fury,* and to describe the main thematic and formal characteristics of his work. Conrad Aiken, for example, in an invaluable essay of 1939, proposes that Faulkner's idiosyncratic style—with its endless sentences and vocabulary of certain obsessive words—contributed indispensably to the author's interest in the continuum of past and present, to the reader's necessary sense of immersion in the flow of time. Two years later Warren Beck identified Faulkner's ability to combine realistic colloquialism with lyric extravagance as a central technique of the novel; Beck shows how Faulkner's narratives consistently seek "to render the transcendent life of the mind, the crowded composite of associative and analytical consciousness which expands the vibrant moment into the reaches of all time" (Beck 1941, 62).

One other decisive critical treatment of Faulkner's major fiction throughout the 1930s concentrates on the continuities of Faulkner's fictional themes from novel to novel. George Marion O'Donnell, in "Faulkner's Mythology" (1939), spells out an overarching social allegory he sees in Faulkner's Yoknapatawpha novels. Put briefly, this allegory portrays the modernization of the South and the loss of a unifying moral and cultural tradition. The conflict appears in Yoknapatawpha as the struggle between the Sartorises and the Snopeses, who stand respectively for southern tradition and its modern successor. The Compson family takes its place in this interpretation as representatives of a false because decadent version of the genuine Sartoris tradition. Though O'Donnell vastly simplifies Faulkner's attitudes toward the historical processes of the New South, his essay gives weight to the sociological import of Faulkner's fiction, an attribute undervalued by those more interested in Faulkner's modernistic literary techniques.

By 1939 Faulkner's reputation secured him election to the National Institute of Arts and Letters, yet sales of his novels were so poor that none of his books except *Sanctuary* was even in print by 1945. The critic Malcolm Cowley undertook to convince Viking Press to issue an anthology of Faulkner's fiction. Known as the Viking Portable Faulkner, part of a series of volumes excerpting the work of major writers, it appeared in 1946; Faulkner won a National Book Award in 1950 for his *Collected Stories;* and he was awarded the Nobel Prize for Literature the same year. These events signaled Faulkner's public entry into the company of writers to which he had aspired when he thought about Flaubert and Dostoyevsky twenty years earlier while composing *The Sound and the Fury.* Cowley's introduction to *The Portable Faulkner* still serves as an elegantly succinct overview of Faulkner's characteristic subject matter.

Even more important, Cowley opened a correspondence with the reticent Faulkner about the Viking volume and not only received the author's blessing for the project, but also enlisted him to write an introduction to *The Sound and the Fury* that would provide supplemental information for the reader. This material eventually became far more than the headnote it was intended to be; rather, Faulkner wrote a detailed account of the Compson family's genealogy and history beyond 1928. This document is known as the Compson Appendix, and since 1946 has normally been published along with the text of the original novel. Noel Polk's reedition of *The Sound and the Fury* eliminates the appendix, and readers should now be able to see more clearly how Faulkner's supplement to the novel invites the reader to deal with two texts—one including it and one excluding it. (The Compson Appendix is reprinted in the Norton Critical edition.) I will have more to say about this situation in a later section.

A READING

4

reading the characters

Understanding *The Sound and the Fury* would not be nearly so demanding a task if Faulkner's strategy had been to describe his characters outwardly and have them speak for themselves and to each other. Had Faulkner chosen to work like his great forebears in the realistic tradition—Dostoyevsky, Dickens, Balzac, or even Henry James, all of whose fiction he knew—the characters of *The Sound and the Fury* would have appeared more directly accessible to the reader. The effect might have been like that of starting with the last section of the novel, in which the surviving Compsons and Gibsons are described by an unidentified narrating voice, which creates at least the illusion of omniscience of what the characters think and say, and about what happens.

In contrast, the first three sections of *The Sound and the Fury* are told from the standpoints and in the voices of each of the three Compson brothers, as if each brother is telling his section to an assumed audience, or at least speaking it aloud to himself. Faulkner's technique aims to render three particular ways of looking at the world. Each of these ways is itself highly personalized and distinctly eccentric; you can hardly imagine three more extreme world visions: the dumb, mentally retarded, and castrated youngest brother, Benjy; the idealistic, gentlemanly, eldest son of a southern aristocratic family and a student at the Yankee Harvard University, Quentin; the resentful, paranoiac, and mean-spirited middle brother, hardware store clerk and small-town southern bigot, Jason. Each of the first three sections of the novel attempts to create the world perceived and inhabited by these three individuals. Though they share the experience of region and family, and though they all turn out to express their longings and disappointments through the figure of their absent sister Caddy, their preoccupations and manners of expression are radically different.

To create the sensation of being inside his characters' minds, Faulkner relies on many innovative stylistic and structural devices. I will discuss these matters more fully in a section to follow, but for the moment it is worth saying that the sheer sentence-to-sentence complexity of the novel—especially the first section—is deliberate and presents as many difficulties and anxieties for experienced (and even "professional") readers as for inexperienced ones. Our main task will be to try to understand how Faulkner wants to train us to read in an unfamiliar way. He may do this not only because he wishes to demonstrate the important differences in the way humans grasp reality, but also because *The Sound and the Fury* probes what it means to use words in the first place. Faulkner considers the gap between making sense of our world through words and recognizing that some essence of experience seems to escape representation. The novel wonders about how speech grows out of loss and longing, how language both desires and prevents true communion.

These matters may seem fairly abstract inferences from the novel at this point; more pressing might be the need simply to decipher Benjy's sentences. But we should bear in mind as we do so that the power of *The Sound and the Fury* arises from Faulkner's experiments with characterization. The technical stunts we encounter serve the goal of allowing us to inhabit a mind like Benjy's, to imagine the world as he possesses it.

William Faulkner about age eight atop his pony. His two younger brothers and cousin sit on the front steps of the Falkner family home in Oxford, Mississippi.

BENJY

Benjy's world has been punctured by loss. From his section's first scene through its last, Benjy is tormented by the sensation of loss, and struggles to rectify or replace what is missing. The puzzling opening scene of *The Sound and the Fury* initiates the reader into the preoccupation of Benjy's mind as it shows the man-child and his black caretaker, Luster, "hunting" for a lost quarter. The fourteen-year-old grandson of the Compsons' servant, Dilsey Gibson, Luster finds spare change hard to come by in Jefferson, Mississippi, in 1928. Luster's anxiety over his loss arises from his fear that he will be unable to attend the traveling circus show that evening (3). But Benjy's experience of Luster's misfortune tangles up with some kind of associated disturbance in his mind. We notice that he and Luster look for the quarter along a fence that borders a golf course. Benjy describes the men "hitting" and replacing the flag in the hole (3). As they play, the golfers periodically call for their caddies. After Benjy first records what he hears, he seems to begin making a noise. Luster scolds him, "Listen at you, now. . . . Aint you something, thirty-three years old, going on that way"—Benjy's apparent bellowing or moaning erupts despite the prospect of his birthday celebration (3).

This is the sort of scene that presents difficulty for any reader because the information we need to interpret it does not appear until later in Benjy's section. Faulkner delays us as we try to make sense of Benjy's mind, in part to create the sensation of an idiot's world. We are always fighting to find a frame of reference, a scheme, that will organize sense impressions. Because Benjy cannot reason abstractly, his experience seems a flood of chaotically unrelated sensations and images. As we will see, a very primitive logic of loss does govern his world—governs both what he notices and how he processes it. But before we can read this logic, we must suffer a kind of sympathetic disorientation as we move from our world into the world of the novel.

The novel cuts from the opening scene to one that Benjy apparently recalls from his childhood. As he and Luster stoop through a break in the fence, Benjy gets caught on a protruding nail (4). When he emerges from the other side, the narrative has travelled through time to an earlier moment when Benjy has caught himself. This time, however, his sister Caddy has been looking after him. For a paragraph or two Benjy relives this instant, and then he moves still further backward to recall the circumstances of crawling with Caddy through the fence from the Compson property to a neighbor's grounds. The technique of shifting from one of Benjy's remembered time zones to another—without warning or transition of any sort—constitutes Faulkner's strategy for showing how Benjy remains innocent of the abstraction of passing time. Benjy does not envision a personal time line on which every event takes its consecutive place, earlier events fading and recent ones remaining fresh. Rather, every moment impressed onto his consciousness survives as a vivid cluster of images and sensations. As a result, fragments of his whole life remain intensely present to Benjy. But at the same time he can never master his sense of loss or comprehend the workings of time and their effect on his identity. Benjy stands at the mercy of whatever associations have been forged in his mind.

From a perspective developed by knowing the whole novel, the reader is in a position to understand the principle of these associations. Since we learn, for example, that Benjy's beloved and now departed older sister is named Caddy (4), we might realize that to Benjy's ears the golfers are calling her name. He hears their cry as a reminder of his sister's absence, and he responds by bellowing in a manner that becomes his hallmark throughout the novel. Luster confirms this interpretation when he taunts Benjy some time later: "'Beller.' Luster said. 'Beller. You want something to beller about. All right, then. Caddy.' he whispered. 'Caddy. Beller now. Caddy'" (63). Because he has no way to deploy a different frame of reference for these two words—one appropriate for the game he watches, the other for the name of his sister—Benjy mishears a difference as an identity. His world tends toward the simplicity of binarism: objects are either absent or present (each object either in Benjy's possession or not); words are either said or unsaid (each sound possesses one and only one meaning).

Still later in the novel, we learn that the golf course Benjy and Luster hunt beside once belonged to the Compson family. Formerly one of Jefferson's leading families, the Compsons have seen their fortune, if not their standing, decline in the modern South. To fulfill Mrs. Compson's dream of sending her eldest son to prestigious Harvard University—a common determination among generations of socially prominent southerners—the family has decided to sell some of its land. The part of the property sold to the golf course developers would have been Benjy's birthright (and thus it is referred to as Benjy's pasture). Quentin remembers in his section how Benjy dimly apprehended this loss: "We have sold Benjy's *He lay on the ground under the window, bellowing. We have sold Benjy's pasture so that Quentin may go to Harvard* a brother to you" (108). In the first lines of *The Sound and the Fury*, then, Faulkner embeds the logic of loss that rules Benjy's mind. Luster's missing quarter serves as an emblem for the dispossessions Benjy has suffered. Deprived of the tender care of his sister, Caddy, fenced away from the pasture he once played in, undergoing (though never comprehending) the larger losses of fortune and prestige endured by his family, Benjy comes into existence in the novel as the embodiment of a primitive response to loss.

I have lingered over the initial scene of the novel to demonstrate Faulkner's method. What seems at first a heap of images, sensations, and spoken remarks swirling through an idiot's mind,—and, sadly, remains so for readers who fail to go on—turns out to be a carefully designed mosaic representing the state of bereavement and responses to it. In later remarks about *The Sound and the Fury* Faulkner suggests (and perhaps even overstates) the absoluteness of Benjy's experience of loss: Benjy "could not remember his sister but only the loss of her" and "remembered not the pasture but only its loss" (Appendix, NCE, 234, 235).

From the first indirectly spoken word of the novel—"caddie"/ Caddy—Benjy's world reels with the loss of his sister. Three years older than her mentally retarded youngest brother, Candace Compson has taken on the role of nursemaid and protector for Benjy through their childhood. Benjy is unequipped to deal with any but the simplest events in his life, so Caddy helps him dress, explains his surroundings to him ("Ice. That means how cold it is" [14]); tries to interpret his garbled speech ("What is it. What are you trying to tell Caddy" [7]); and even soothes Benjy at night by sleeping in his bed ("Caddy held me and I could hear us all, and the darkness, and something I could smell" [85]).

Caddy's devotion to Benjy means all the more to him in view of his mother's remoteness. Caroline Compson shrinks from the realization that her family and community stand on the verge of irreversible losses. In Benjy's section she appears as a weak, self-centered hypochondriac. I will have more to say about how Mrs. Compson's plight embodies many of the failures of her tradition's attitudes toward women, but for the moment we should take Benjy's viewpoint and notice his mother's coldness toward him. Early in his section he remembers her pitying touch:

"Someday I'll be gone, and you'll have to think for him." *Now stomp* Versh said. "Come here and kiss Mother, Benjamin."

> Caddy took me to Mother's chair and Mother took my face in her hands and then she held me against her.
> "My poor baby." she said. She let me go. "You and Versh take good care of him, honey."
> . . .
> "You're not a poor baby. Are you. You've got your Caddy. Haven't you got your Caddy." (9–10)

Even in this moment of unusual attention from Mrs. Compson, Benjy's care becomes another's responsibility, and he becomes an object that reflects Mrs. Compson's self-pity. Caddy nominates herself to occupy the position Mrs. Compson has abdicated. Faulkner once remarked that Benjy "knew that [Caddy] loved him and would defend him, and so she was the whole world to him" (*University*, 64); André Bleikasten echoes this idea in saying that "Caddy is definitely a mother surrogate; it is she who replaced Mrs. Compson, the failing mother" (Bleikasten 1976, 78).

Mrs. Compson simply cannot bear the prospect that her world will no longer behave according to the traditions of leisure and authority she thinks are her due. Mrs. Compson takes pride that her family, the Bascombs, "are every bit as well born" as the Compson family into which she marries (50). She honors her own brother Maury by naming her youngest son after him. Yet when it becomes clear that this child is an idiot, and no suitable heir to either family, Mrs. Caroline Compson insists that his name be changed to Benjamin. When Benjy is five he loses his given name. Caddy repeats the logic of this change to Dilsey: *"Benjamin came out of the bible, Caddy said. It's a better name for him than Maury was"* (66). Dilsey remains doubtful: *"[f]olks dont have no luck, changing names"* (67).

Mrs. Compson's irritation with Benjy in part derives from his symbolizing the decline in Compson fortune, prestige, and hopes. Criticizing Caddy for humoring the five-year-old Benjy too much, she refuses to allow him to sit on her lap, declines to hold him, insists on using his formal name and not Caddy's endearing nickname, and maintains that Benjamin "must learn to mind" (73). Throughout Benjy's section we see the blows fall on the Compson family—Grandmother (Damuddy) dies, Mr. Compson dies; Caddy gets pregnant and must be married off; Quentin commits suicide; Benjy attacks a neighbor girl and is castrated to neutralize his sexual urges; Caddy's husband repudiates her when he discovers he is not her child's father; the child (a girl named Quentin, after Caddy's brother) comes to live with the broken family; and Uncle Maury skids from one scheme to another, draining money from the depleted family treasury. Even this partial list of misfortunes suggests how completely the Compson family buckles, a collapse that drives Mrs. Compson to her bed and the refuge of self-pity. It is no wonder Benjy fails to enjoy her nurture.

If in childhood Benjy's mind must have been tranquilized by Caddy's presence, in 1928, at the age of thirty-three, Benjy remains forlorn because of her disappearance eighteen years earlier. From Quentin's section we know that Caddy and Herbert Head marry in April of 1910 (Quentin muses on the wording of the wedding invitation [106]). Benjy recalls the wedding reception at the Compson house several times during his section. The scenes tumble with disjointed images and sensations: T. P., younger son of Dilsey and Roskus, has gotten his charge (Benjy) and himself tipsy on the champagne served at the party, and Quentin comes out of the house to rescue Benjy. But the dominant sensation of the scene is Benjy's prolonged agony; he remembers crying throughout the reception. One might infer that his intoxication terrifies him because he cannot understand his disorientation. But the scene that follows upon this flashback suggests that the underlying cause of Benjy's disturbance is his apprehension that Caddy will be leaving him.

The wedding memory cuts away to an earlier moment (Benjy still has his original name), when the children have been sent out of the main house because an event that they should not witness is taking place. Benjy probably associates these two events because both exclude him, and he finds himself entrusted to a caretaker whose job is keeping him out of the way. In the second recalled scene, the event transpiring is Damuddy's funeral. When the children come back inside for supper (26ff.), they notice the absence of adults, and Caddy volunteers to "sit in Damuddy's chair" (26). Caddy fills this vacancy in more ways than one, since her disappearance in the novel is suffered as a kind of death by both Benjy and Quentin, the brothers who feel closest to her. Benjy remembers that the evening carries mysterious sounds from above to them—the weeping and singing of the ceremony make the children wonder if there is not a "party" taking place. Yet the older ones begin to realize what is happening, and Caddy and Jason try to explain to each other what a funeral is (37–38).

The logic of loss organizes Benjy's mind in such a way that Caddy's wedding and Damuddy's funeral intertwine. Shortly after these scenes, Benjy recalls still another scene that confirms this pattern. That scene centers on the hour before the funeral begins, when the children playing outside begin to wonder what the adults must be doing inside. Caddy decides to climb a tree beside the parlor window while her brothers and the Gibson children stare up wonderingly as she disappears into the branches: "We watched the muddy bottom of her drawers. Then we couldn't see her. We could hear the tree thrashing" (44). As Caddy bravely looks on the scene of death, her brothers wait below. Benjy's recollection confuses images from Caddy's wedding day: T. P. has gotten into the sarsaparilla during the funeral too, so Benjy follows that thread between the moments. But Caddy's position in the funeral scene grows indistinguishable from her position in the wedding scene: "'What you seeing.' Frony whispered. / *I saw them. Then I saw Caddy, with flowers in her hair, and a long veil like shining wind. Caddy Caddy*" (44–45). Notice how Benjy simply slips from one moment of loss to another. This is a perfect example of the way in which Benjy's associations structure his entire section. If we learn his preoccupations, we can understand the reasons he moves from one fragmentary recollection to the next.

Two other kinds of memories surface in Benjy's sustained meditation on Caddy's loss. One set involves all those anticipations of her permanent absence; the second set includes attempts to return Caddy to his world. At least in retrospect, Benjy has been remarkably alert to indications that Caddy will grow up and away from the family. Jason notices that Caddy's preference for "prissy" dresses at the age of fourteen upsets Benjy (46); Benjy cries when Caddy wears perfume and disappears into the arms of her adolescent boyfriends (55); and he lets us appreciate the emblematic quality of the mud on Caddy's drawers, the image that signifies her sexual "contamination." Not only does Benjy focus on Caddy's muddy bottom in the tree, he recalls that Dilsey seems particularly upset because the stain has "done soaked clean through onto you" (85). The marks of sexual maturation—whether the bloodstains of menstruation or the simple mud of human flesh—appear in the image of Caddy's muddy drawers. The boys look upward toward the mysterious origin of human life and sexual knowledge, which in Benjy's innocence can be presented only as pollution. Caddy scrubs her mouth hard with soap to convince Benjy that she is through with make-up and kissing and perfume (55), just as Dilsey scours her very body to eradicate the signs of her immersion in the flow of the muddy stream, where Caddy alone is brave enough to sit down in the waters that symbolize time, death, and fertility.

That sexuality and death should be associated in Benjy's mind points to a markedly Faulknerian intuition. To Benjy, Caddy's growing interest in her body and in males outside the family signals her eventual death to him. He cries so pitifully at Caddy's adolescent awakenings that she offers to postpone them. Returning to the house after seeing one of her young men, Caddy wonders whether Benjy has not thought her absence permanent: "'Did you find Caddy again.' She said. 'Did you think Caddy had run away.' Caddy smelled like trees" (48). At this moment Caddy gives her perfume away to Dilsey to seal her renunciation of adulthood, but of course we know from the subsequent events already referred to in Benjy's section that she will once more replace the fragrance of trees with perfume, and will finally run away.

Benjy connects this ultimate disappearance with the scene in the creek branch he has witnessed earlier. Playing with her brothers and the Gibson boys, Caddy takes her dress off and steps into the water. Quentin tries to stop her, and finally she slips: "Caddy was all wet and muddy behind, and I started to cry and she came and squatted in the water" (21). Benjy cries because Caddy threatens to "run away and never come back" if Quentin blocks her wishes. Benjy's mind associates this literal undressing with a more serious sort when he recalls the discussion of death prompted by Damuddy's funeral. At that time the children decide that the state of being dead is exemplified by the time their mare fell into a ditch and had to be destroyed; then "the buzzards came and undressed her" (38). Jason takes fright at this grisly prospect for his beloved grandmother, and the children agree that Father would never let such a thing happen. But in the symbolic work of the novel, the image of undressing unites Caddy's defection from her brothers with the experience of mortality. The association of sex and death may be considered from a number of standpoints. Freud's theories of incestuous desire and mourning will help us when we take up this question in Quentin's section. But we will also be able to put this connection in a larger social and historical context as well since Caddy represents an ideal of purity and nurture that males in the New South thought they were about to lose forever.

The second category of memories represents the efforts Benjy has made to restore Caddy to his world once she has gone. With his primitive resources for expression, Benjy tries to organize a response to loss. We know, for example, that he has accumulated a hoard of special mementos—broken bottles, bunches of weeds and flowers, one of Caddy's old slippers—that seem to soothe him as tangible substitutions for his many losses. During the day his section is narrated, 7 April 1928, Dilsey charges Luster with keeping Benjy out of the way while she prepares his birthday cake. Resenting this duty, Luster teases his "looney" by pretending to take away Benjy's flowers. Predictably, when Benjy howls at this dispossession Luster hastens to restore them: "Here they is. Look. It's fixed back just like it was at first. Hush, now" (63). The pity of Benjy's world, of course, is that things can never be fixed back again just like they were at first.

The hope of fixing things surfaces even more pronouncedly in other aspects of Benjy's behavior. One of the more puzzling scenes in his section involves his practice of shuffling along the fence as schoolchildren walk by each afternoon. Benjy has developed this habit after Caddy's marriage, even though T. P. tries to point out its futility: "*You cant do no good looking through the gate, T. P. said. Miss Caddy done gone long ways away. Done got married and left you. You cant do no good, holding to the gate and crying. She cant hear you*" (58–59). On one fateful day when the gate has not been properly fastened Benjy manages to chase one of the passing schoolgirls. In the context we have been developing, Benjy clearly means to substitute the little Burgess girl for the Caddy he may never have again. By standing at the gate Benjy hopes eternally that someday Caddy will walk back through, as if she has just been gone for the morning. Given popular fears of the sexual urges of the mentally retarded, however, the neighbors (and probably even the Compsons) interpret the event as a sexual assault. The result, as the Compson Appendix confirms, is Benjy's castration. Benjy confuses grabbing the girl and the subsequent surgery in a way that proves very illuminating: "They came on. I opened the gate and they stopped, turning. I was trying to say, and I caught her, trying to say, and she screamed and I was trying to say and trying and the bright shapes began to stop and I tried to get out. I tried to get it off of my face, but the bright shapes were going again. They were going up the hill to where it fell away and I tried to cry" (60–61). Here the crime is the punishment, for Benjy reaches out to the little girl as she vanishes over the hill; her elusiveness suggests the torture Caddy's absence imposes on Benjy. During the surgical procedure, the anesthesia (probably ether) is administered through a mask, which Benjy remembers as muffling his effort to speak just before he loses consciousness. What is Benjy trying to say?

The reader is in a position to see that Benjy's many misunderstood gestures attempt to express and alleviate his loss. Because Benjy never learns to talk, his voice manages only wails and bellows of discontent. Caddy often recognizes that Benjy's fumbling and moaning indicate rudimentary efforts to communicate. When one of her boyfriends begins to make sexual advances in Benjy's presence, he discounts the idiot's danger: "He cant talk" (54). But Caddy makes him stop because Benjy "can see" (54). This exchange precisely measures Benjy's plight: he witnesses loss but cannot reply to it. Benjy's idiocy is a form of arrested development that excludes him from language. He is the perpetual infant; or, as one character puts it, Benjy has "been three years old thirty years" (19). The term "infant" derives from the Latin words for "without speech"; and Benjy does represent the infancy of the imagination.

Faulkner has begun his novel with the simplest workings of the mind. Benjy represents the human effort to establish an identity in the face of separation from the mother, to maintain stability despite the onrush of time and loss, to interpret experience without ever being free of our own preoccupations and limitations. Benjy's story may be a "tale told by an idiot," but it is one that serves as a "prologue" (*Lion*, 245) to the successively more sophisticated and mature efforts to tell the same story, to try to say.

QUENTIN

As we turn from the first to the second section of *The Sound and the Fury*, we may wonder to what extent this new portion will continue the narrative of the last. The final lines of the first section show us Benjy, soothed at last by the return of Caddy to his bed, falling asleep as "the dark began to go in smooth, bright shapes" (85). In the next "chapter" our text resumes with a narrator awakening to a shadow—a daytime shape of darkness—moving across his curtains in the morning. Yet the section's title, "June Second, 1910," tells us that this day of the novel occurs almost eighteen years earlier, and by the second sentence we realize that this scene does not open another day in Benjy's life, but opens onto the world of a new narrator, the eldest Compson brother, Quentin.

Even by this point in our reading of the novel, we should not be surprised to find Faulkner organizing the narrative by breaks or disruptions. This has been the method of Benjy's section, and it governs the relation between units within each section as well as between the sections themselves. It is as if the loss of Caddy—and the family unity and social coherence her loss embodies—has buckled the very structure of the novel that represents this disruption.

Like his younger brother, Quentin appears to be at the mercy of upheaval, yet his responses are far more complex than those of the perpetual three-year-old. Compared to Benjy, Quentin understands Caddy's transgression of their society's codes of behavior in both more personal and more symbolic terms. Quentin suffers Caddy's loss as the corruption of their innocence; on the day of her wedding, Quentin recalls, he saw her *"running out of the mirror the smells roses roses the voice that breathed o'er Eden"* (92). In their childhood intimacy, Quentin's sister has been his very mirror image—his feminine complement, the soul mate with whom he shares the paradise of innocence. At the same time, Quentin also knows that Caddy's loss represents the excruciating constants of all human experience—the doom of mortality, the certainty of historical change.

In ways that recall Benjy's visceral ache for Caddy, Quentin yearns to recover the physical and psychological intimacies of childhood. In Quentin's eyes, Caddy's pregnancy signifies her awful lapse from innocence—a lapse he experiences as a personal betrayal. At first Quentin hardly grasps what Caddy is telling him about her condition:

> *I'm sick you'll have to promise*
> *Sick how are you sick*
> *I'm just sick I cant ask anybody yet promise you will* (127)

Caddy knows that the code of southern propriety ruling her world will demand that she be sent away to avoid disgracing her family. In this exchange with Quentin she wants her brother to promise that the family will not send Benjy to the state mental asylum in Jackson, Mississippi, as soon as he is deprived of her nurture and defense (128). But Quentin takes in Caddy's meaning as it affects him; Caddy is sick unto death because she has been touched by the sexual possession of another: *"did you love them Caddy did you love them When they touched me I died"* (171).

When Caddy says she "dies" under the touch of her lovers, she refers to her sexual excitement, and perhaps indirectly to the thrill of defying the repressive morality of southern gentility. (At one point she makes Quentin feel how her pulse races when he pronounces her first lover's name aloud [187].) But for Quentin, Caddy's intercourse marks the death of childhood, the silencing of "the voice that breathed o'er Eden." We may begin to see why Quentin's section is haunted by the spectre of premature death—from his early reference to "Little Sister Death" (87) to his own pathetic decision to commit suicide.

Faulkner carries forward an image from Benjy's section to convey the contamination of childhood brought on by Caddy's behavior. Quentin, too, recalls the scene of Damuddy's funeral when Caddy partially disrobes and plays in the muddy water of the branch. Quentin's diseased recoil from adulthood leads him to equate sexuality and filth. In the following remembered scene Caddy seems to have surprised the virginal Quentin as he experiments sexually with a neighbor girl; Quentin tries to arouse a jealousy in Caddy to match his:

> *I was hugging her that's what I was doing. She turned her back I went around in front of her. I was hugging her I tell you.*
>   *I dont give a damn what you were doing*
>   *You dont you dont I'll make you I'll make you give a damn. She hit my hands away I smeared mud on her with the other hand.*
> (157)

Only Quentin cares, and that, as he realizes, is the misfortune of his relation with the bolder Caddy. She accepts the stains of time and separation; he will not.

Quentin's obsession with virginity marks his inability to move from childhood to adulthood. Faulkner's conception of Quentin works so powerfully on readers of *The Sound and the Fury* in part because he is so recognizable as a psychological type. Quentin's predicament depicts, with an exaggeration that makes it all the more revealing, truths about our common nostalgia for childhood, our adolescent fears of sexuality and mortality, and our disbelief at discovering the contradictions and hypocrisies of the standards under which we have been raised. For readers of modern Western literature, Quentin has come to represent a moment in personal development that virtually everyone recognizes and very many experience. He functions as do so many of the characters who impress us vividly in literature: Stephen Dedalus, who blossoms out of the confusion of infantile sensation into the abrasive egoism of individuality (Joyce's *A Portrait of the Artist as Young Man*); Romeo and Juliet, who, in the ecstasy of first love, defy family and society; Emma Bovary, who suffers a perplexed disenchantment with romantic love and marriage;

Pip, who in early middle age describes his resignation to life's destruction of one's "great expectations"; King Lear, who discovers the harsh truth that old age brings enfeeblement, rage, and irrelevance.

Literature teaches us that such moments comprise the plots of our lives. Quentin, in his foundering on the passage between childhood and adulthood, suffers a disorder that suggests much about the difficulties and costs of "normal" maturation. In perhaps the most illuminating analysis of Quentin's psychology we have, John T. Irwin reads Quentin's problems in the light of Freud's theories of psychosexual development (1975). (Freud, too, worked under the assumption that what he learned from his diseased patients could instruct us about the way healthy mental mechanisms operate.) Irwin identifies the root of Quentin's problems as "secondary narcissism": "Quentin's narcissism is, in Freudian terms, a fixation in secondary narcissism, a repetition during a later period in life (usually adolescence) of that primary narcissism that occurs between the sixth and the eighteenth months, wherein the child first learns to identify with its image and thus begins the work that will lead to the constitution of the ego as the image of the self and the object of love" (Irwin 1975, 42).

For a person to mature beyond the phase in which the ego is formed, he or she must transfer love from the self to another. According to Irwin, Quentin fails to do this; he cannot accept the separation between self and other (in Freudian terms, between "subject" and "object" or, in Faulknerian terms, between Quentin and Caddy). Quentin wants to see himself in Caddy (at one point he envisions her "running out of the mirror" toward him [92]). His passion for his sister is actually "the attempt to make the subject the sole object of its own love, to merge the subject and the object in an internal love union" (Irwin 1975, 43). Such an attitude "reveals the goal of all infantile, regressive tendencies, narcissism included: it is the attempt to return to a state in which subject and object did not yet exist, to a time before that division occurred out of which the ego sprang—in short, to return to the womb, to reenter the waters of birth" (Irwin 1975, 43).

I cannot pursue all the implications of Irwin's subtle and difficult argument, in part because his approach involves reading the personality of Quentin Compson as he reappears in *Absalom, Absalom!*, published seven years after *The Sound and the Fury.* (I will have more to say about the relation of these two works in chapter 7.) At this stage in our understanding of Quentin, however, we can see how his anguish at Caddy's defection and his desire to recover the intimacy of childhood might lead Quentin to desperate measures. As he bemoans Caddy's lost virginity, Quentin wonders whether he might not reclaim his sister by losing his own virginity to her. Mr. Compson reports that Quentin "felt driven to the expedient of telling [him] that [he had] committed incest" (203). In Quentin's imagination, the very scandal of such a crime would "isolate her out of the loud world so that it would have to flee us of necessity and then the sound of it would be as though it had never been" (203).

To recover, to regress, Quentin unconsciously draws toward that return to the mother's womb through the only route open to him, his sister's body. Irwin argues that both Benjy and Quentin use Caddy as a substitute for their absent mother; for Benjy, Caddy provides the nurture withheld by the remote Mrs. Compson from the "infant" son; for Quentin, now a sexually able adolescent who has long earlier been forbidden from thinking of the mother as a sexual object, Caddy serves as a replacement. "Thus, Quentin's narcissism is necessarily linked with his incestuous desire for his sister, for . . . brother-sister incest is a substitute for child-parent incest—what the brother seeks in his sister is his mother" (Irwin 1975, 43). Musing on his predicament, Quentin associates these figures: *"Father I have committed . . . My little sister had no. If I could say Mother. Mother"* (108).

Even if we grant this account of Quentin's incestuous longing, we must admit that Quentin's intelligence and morality make it difficult to imagine his simply acting on such a desire. He knows, to begin with, that having actual sexual intercourse with Caddy, even were she willing, would accomplish nothing. In fact, he confesses to his father that he never tried to force her because "i was afraid to i was afraid she might and then it wouldnt have done any good" (203). To repeat the act that brought about the loss of purity will not restore that purity. The emblem of incest represents the adolescent Quentin's

contradictory desire to remain a child and to be initiated into a̶ her
hood—in the same act ("but if i could tell you [Mr. Compson] w or-
it would have been so and then the others wouldnt be so and then un
world would roar away" [203]). The method of Quentin's madnes ing
pends upon tricking himself into believing that he and Caddy can n"
from reality, can pretend as adults to feel as if they were still child a

This approach to his life involves Quentin in a set of ruses he
repertoire of mental and expressive strategies that try to balance an
even obscure the contradictions of his situation. We may notice, fo
example, a number of passages in which Quentin half remembers, half
imagines scenes that express his ambivalent desire. The following exchange between brother and sister shows them on the verge of intimacy, yet the language of the passage seems to describe two distinct
actions. Because Quentin opens his knife and offers to press it into
Caddy, the scene clearly recounts a mutual suicide pact, a terrible solution to Quentin's grief and Caddy's impending disgrace. At the same
time, the scene also reads like a fumbled sexual initiation, beginning,
of course, with their discussion of Quentin's virginity:

> when I lifted my hand I could still feel crisscrossed twigs and grass
> burning into the palm
> poor Quentin
> she leaned back on her arms her hands locked about her knees
> youve never done that have you
> what done what
> that what I have what I did
> yes yes lots of times with lots of girls
> then I was crying her hand touched me again and I was crying
> against her damp blouse then she lying on her back looking past
> my head into the sky I could see a rim of white under her irises I
> opened my knife
> do you remember the day damuddy died when you sat down in the
> water in your drawers
> yes
> I held the point of the knife at her throat
> it wont take but a second just a second then I can do mine I can do
> mine then

all right can you do yours by yourself
yes the blades long enough Benjys in bed by now
yes
it wont take but a second Ill try not to hurt
all right
will you close your eyes
no like this youll have to push it harder
touch your hand to it
but she didnt move her eyes were wide open looking past my head
at the sky
Caddy do you remember how Dilsey fussed at you because your
drawers were muddy
dont cry
Im not crying Caddy
push it are you going to
do you want me to
yes push it
touch your hand to it
dont cry poor Quentin
but I couldnt stop she held my head against her damp hard breast
I could hear her heart going firm and slow now not hammering and
the water gurgling among the willows in the dark and waves of
honeysuckle coming up the air my arm and shoulder were twisted
under me
what is it what are you doing
her muscles gathered I sat up
its my knife I dropped it
she sat up
what time is it
I dont know (173–75)

So many of Quentin's preoccupations appear in this passage that
we may use it to represent the constants of his mind. As I suggested
above, the language of sexuality and the language of death intertwine,
reflecting Quentin's consistent association of the two. For him to lose
his virginity would be to join Caddy in the waters of death (indicated
by Quentin's recall of the Damuddy/muddy drawers episode). Beyond
that, however, Quentin also sees that the act of incest carries the

penalty of death. Freud explains this by pointing out that the fa
represents the law forbidding incest in the family, and that his auth
ity establishes itself by silently communicating the threat of castrati
to the son who would transgress the law. (Irwin notes that accor
to Freud "the fear of death is an analogue of the fear of castrati
[1975, 48]). Quentin's inability to consummate the act appears a
kind of impotence—"its my knife I dropped it" (175). In effect,
must castrate himself with respect to his sister, internalizing the pro
hibition against incest and failing to make real both incest and its pun
ishment by death.

Like his eventual suicide, Quentin's memories betray the unsolv-
able contradictions of his predicament. Just as he smears mud on
Caddy to express his outrage at her befoulment—trying to undo by
redoing (157)—he also tries to restore her virginity by taking it himself, to preserve his own by losing it to her, to purify their lives by
ending his, to defend honor by contemplating an act of perfect shame,
to gain his father's respect by defying him, and to affirm his identity
by dissolving it. For the profoundly personal reasons we have already
discussed, but also in the larger social contexts we will go on to examine, Quentin's loss of Caddy has upended his world. He is left to
resolve the contradictions of a world in which "all stable things had
become shadowy paradoxical all I had done shadows all I had felt
suffered taking visible form antic and perverse mocking without relevance inherent themselves with the denial of the significance they
should have affirmed" (194–95).

The extent to which Quentin's life has been turned "shadowy paradoxical" must be measured against larger frameworks than his sudden separation from his sister. As he awakens in his Harvard
dormitory room, Quentin's first thought associates the progress of the
shadow across his curtains, which indicates the hour, and the ticking
of his watch. The watch reminds him "I was in time again" (86), and
the balance of Quentin's section shows him brooding on the destruc-
tive nature of time. Jammed with the defeated voices of his father and
grandfather, Quentin recalls being given the heirloom watch along
with a piece of paternal advice: "I give you the mausoleum of all hope

and desire. . . . I give it to you not that you may remember time, but that you might forget it now and then for a moment and not spend all your breath trying to conquer it. Because no battle is ever won he said. They are not even fought" (86). Quentin finds himself unable to follow this advice. He spends the rest of his life (the reader sees only this last day of it) hoping to trick time into giving his past back to him, and, finally, deciding to defy time by taking his own life rather than letting time gradually steal it.

Quentin's obsession with time marks one of his main efforts to comprehend the nature of his plight. Time means change and death to Quentin, so he is haunted by symbols of its power. Right after the position of the shadow tells him it is eight o'clock, his roommate Shreve urges him to hurry if he wants to get to class on time. Quentin seems mildly surprised: "I didn't know it was that late" (88). The room fills with the sound of the university bells marking the hour, then Quentin "went to the dresser and took up the watch, with the face still down. [He] tapped the crystal on the corner of the dresser and caught the fragments of glass in [his] hand and put them into the ashtray and twisted the hands off and put them in the tray. The watch ticked on" (91). Quentin knows this is a futile gesture; it symbolizes his empty combat with the tyrant time. He not only cuts his thumb breaking the crystal ("There was a red smear on the dial"), but he goes on to wear this defaced watch the rest of the day. The moment signals time's capacity to wound, and to rule even when it is rebelled against.

Quentin's mind habitually turns his father's generalization that "time is your misfortune" (119) into a set of symbolic images. To him, time is less a concept than the jumble of actual timepieces and chimes that flood his mind. (See Sartre 1955 for a thorough catalog of time imagery.) Likewise, Quentin picks out features of his environment that stand for other aspects of his victimization by time. Throughout his last day, for example, Quentin associates the gulls he sees (as he rides the transit system up and down the Charles River) with the remote hope of transcending time: "A gull on an invisible wire attached through space dragged. You carry the symbol of your frustration into eternity" (119). Or notice how Quentin envies his classmate Gerald

Bland, who as he rows his scull on the river seems to lift toward the timelessness of the gull: "all things rushing. Except Gerald. He would be sort of grand too, pulling in lonely state across the noon, rowing himself right out of noon, up the long bright air like an apotheosis, mounting into a drowsing infinity where only he and the gull, the one terrifically motionless, the other in a steady and measured pull and recover that partook of inertia itself, the world punily beneath their shadows on the sun" (138).

Quentin's shadow, however, falls back toward earth. Another image for his combat with time, the shadow stalks Quentin's tracks through his entire section. "Time, flesh, death, all of Quentin's obsessions intersect in the shadow image," one critic has written (Bleikasten 1976, 125). Quentin tells time by the shadow, as we have seen: "But the shadow of the sash was still there and I had learned to tell almost to the minute" (87). Quentin's own shadow marks his physical presence in the world, a presence that casts him under the domain of mortality. Quentin constantly tramples on his shadow, as if in furious denial of his bodiedness, and as he approaches the desperation of suicide, he even tries to leave his shadow behind: "The wall went into shadow, and then my shadow, I had tricked it again" (153–54). The shadowy paradox, however, is that the only way Quentin can imagine separating himself from the shadow of his body is to destroy both. The irony of suicide will frustrate even his last act, as he suggests in recalling a piece of folk wisdom: "Niggers say a drowned man's shadow was watching for him in the water all the time" (102).

So far we have said little about the confusing organization of Quentin's section, except to note that it makes the same quick cuts as Benjy's. We are now in a position to see how Quentin's obsession makes his entire past the antic "shadow" of his present, and so opens his mind to startling pivots between current perceptions and distant recollections. The reader needs time to get used to these shifts between various mental "time zones," which are perhaps the most disorienting feature of Quentin's section. It is as if Faulkner had laid out both Benjy's and Quentin's sections like a floor, with boards of different woods and grains laid end to end without transition; or as if a stream suddenly changed colors as we watched it flow. Even if we learn how to follow the procedure in Benjy's section, Quentin's makes things a little more difficult; his mind ranges over a much greater quantity of material—the snippets of his reading, the diversity of people he has met both in the South and at Harvard during his first year, the vividly recalled moments associated with the turbulence of adolescence and early manhood.

In addition, Quentin's fixation on Caddy affects all of his mental processes, and thus he both interprets everyday reality and remembers his past through the lens of this single relationship. As a result, we can never be sure how much of any recorded scene is memory, fantasy, or recollection under revision. Perhaps the most famous example is the concluding conversation between Mr. Compson and Quentin, in which Quentin announces the fictional incest and implies his determination to commit suicide while Mr. Compson tries to cool his son's ardor and recommends waiting out grief. The form of the passage blurs the usual distinctions between voices in dialogue; rather, Quentin seems to be recalling the scene. We may notice that Mr. Compson sounds much more sympathetic to his son's misfortune (though resistant to Quentin's proposed solution) than we may have expected from earlier scenes, in which he appears deeply cynical—paralyzed by despair when he has not already been immobilized by liquor. Perhaps the Mr. Compson of the concluding conversation is half Quentin's projection, as if he could manufacture the "memory" of the sort of father who might have saved him from himself. When Faulkner was once asked by a student about this confusing episode, he admitted that in his view the scene had never taken place at all (*University*, 262–63).

How does the past shoot through Quentin's present? How do we interpret the entanglement of recollected and immediate events? As for Benjy, there is a logic of loss that makes the movement of Quentin's mind coherent, even if it is not usual. I would like to demonstrate the method of entanglement by looking closely at two packed scenes, moments in Quentin's section that show how his mind instantaneously translates the present into reenactments of the past.

The first of these episodes is precipitated by Gerald Bland's behavior during the afternoon of Quentin's last day. Having missed class, Quentin has been invited to join Gerald, his mother (on one of her numerous visits to Harvard from their native Kentucky), several young women, and Shreve (Quentin's roommate) for a picnic. Quentin will eventually cross their path, but not before he wanders on the subway and interurban trolley lines for several hours and has his run-in with the little Italian girl and her outraged brother Julio. What impresses Quentin most about Gerald is his swagger, his boastfulness about his sexual prowess bathed in his mother's admiring approval. Quentin thinks of the Blands as a caricature of southern noblesse oblige. Of course, Quentin has come far enough away from the South to see that such pretension is ridiculous, although readers of *Absalom, Absalom!* will note that Rosa Coldfield proves that such behavior was no figment of imagination.

Quentin concocts a very funny anecdote that ridicules Gerald's representation of southern myths of gentility. The Mississippian thinks of how he and Shreve (a Canadian) have been regaled with preposterous stories about Gerald's splendid figure in the world:

> As I remember that the next one is to be how Gerald throws his nigger downstairs and how the nigger plead to be allowed to matriculate in the divinity school to be near marster marse gerald and How he ran all the way to the station beside the carriage with tears in his eyes when marse gerald rid away I will wait until the day for the one about the sawmill husband came to the kitchen door with a shotgun Gerald went down and bit the gun in two and handed it back and wiped his hands on a silk handkerchief threw the handkerchief in the stove I've only heard that one twice (122)

Quentin mocks the Blands' blindness to the racism left over from obsolete plantation behavior, and turns Gerald into the hero of a sexual tall tale—a kind of Paul Bunyan of the libido. Gerald behaves like an inflated version of the dashing southern gentleman Quentin is too smart and too weak to be.

As this scene begins (120), the prose twists together strands of separate narratives:

> Telling us about Gerald's women in a *Quentin has shot Herbert he shot his voice through the floor of Caddy's room* tone of smug approbation. "When he was seventeen I said to him one day 'What a shame that you should have a mouth like that it should be on a girls face' and can you imagine *the curtains leaning in on the twilight upon the odour of the apple tree her head against the twilight her arms behind her head kimono-winged the voice that breathed o'er eden clothes upon the bed by the nose seen above the apple* what he said? just seventeen, mind. 'Mother' he said 'it often is.'" (120–21)

As Mrs. Bland tells her appreciative anecdote, Quentin's mind curls back toward that primal scene of Caddy's loss. He thinks first of his hatred of Herbert Head, the man who marries Caddy without knowing she is pregnant. Then the talismanic properties of the moment of the "fall" return: the time of twilight, always indicative in the novel of an apparently timeless instant between daylight and dark; the apple tree that points to the tree Caddy climbs down from her bedroom to join her lovers secretly and that evokes the mythical tree under which Eden is lost to Adam and Eve; the recumbent body of Caddy, in a posture receptive to a lover's possession, kimono-winged because that garment carries a highly erotic charge in Faulkner's world (both as a fashion in the 1920s and in the novel: Caddy's daughter wears a kimono that conceals too little of her willing body).

This last short passage exemplifies the larger rhythms and themes organizing the scene in which it appears. Gerald, "sitting there in attitudes regal watching two or three of them [several admiring female members of the picnic group] through his eyelashes" (121), represents to Quentin the very opposite of his own social and sexual inhibitions. A moment later, Quentin fades away from this recent impression of Gerald to an imagined/remembered interview between Herbert Head and himself. Set in the Compsons' parlor, the exchange reflects

Quentin's overwhelming sense of displacement and impotence in the face of Caddy's impending marriage. Quentin tries to stage a showdown with Head (as he does later with another of Caddy's lovers, Dalton Ames, in the fantastic scene on the bridge, when Quentin "heard myself saying Ill give you until sundown to leave town" and succeeds not in chasing the gun-toting Ames away but only in having "passed out like a girl" [182–87]).

Meditated violence triggers the scene with Head: "*shot him through the* I saw you come in here so I watched my chance and came along thought we might get acquainted have a cigar" (123). Earlier, though, Quentin imagines only having "*shot Herbert he shot his voice through the floor of Caddy's room*" (120); that is, the whole scene of hostility to follow remains a voiced violence, Quentin's uttered protest against Caddy's marriage and his loss. The details of the scene subtly indicate Quentin's preoccupations. Notice how Head repeatedly points to the peculiarly intense relation between his intended and her brother: "I was hit pretty hard see soon as I saw the little girl I dont mind telling you it never occurred to me it was her brother she kept talking about she couldn't have talked about you any more if you'd been the only man in the world husband wouldn't have been in it" (123). Quentin takes Head's intended flattery simply as deeper evidence of the injustice he will suffer.

Head also tries to ingratiate himself by appealing to their common college (both "sons of old Harvard" [125]), but Quentin fires back with a piece of gossip about some scandal that has shadowed Head's undergraduate years ("I was just unlucky you might have been luckier," Head replies [124]). This St. Louis banker also seeks to bribe Quentin by offering him a start in a career ("there's no future in a hole like this for a young fellow like you" [124]), and by pressing cash on Quentin to take care of his "manly" needs ("I know how it is with a young fellow he has lots of private affairs it's always pretty hard to get the old man to stump up for" [126]). "To hell with your money," Quentin answers shortly (126).

Quentin shapes this scene in his memory so as to display his fierce, if futile, defense of honor and propriety. He knows he is infantile and petulant, yet he can do nothing to free himself from the prison of his pathology. After Caddy has asked for a few moments alone with her brother, the interview ends with Herbert's scornful departure: "Well all right then I suppose you and bubber do want to see one another once more eh. . . . dont let Quentin do anything he cant finish" (126–27). Quentin lets Herbert have the last word in their combat, a sure indication that he accepts his mortification as a child, a little "bubber" like Benjy, who howls at dispossession and can only threaten the act—either the process of resignation or the gesture of protest through incest—that he can never finish.

If Quentin remains little brother in this scene with Head, Caddy reappears as little sister in another. As Quentin wanders around Cambridge and Boston on his last day, repeatedly drawn toward the bridge and river where he will drown himself (see Samway [1986] on Quentin's itinerary, and Kinney's volume [1982] for another opinion of where this takes place], he meets "a little dirty child" (143) in a bakery. "Hello, sister," he greets her, and from that point the child becomes Quentin's silent companion for much of his afternoon. At first Quentin feels sorry for the obviously poor immigrant girl; though the bakery proprietor complains about "[t]hem foreigners" (144), Quentin gently defends her and treats her to a bun to go with the nickel loaf of bread she has been sent to buy.

Continuing to call her "sister," Quentin soon intertwines the present with the past, as he does throughout his section. The thought of a buggy crosses his mind as he tries to lead the girl toward her home, and opens a gap that fills with the sensation of losing Caddy:

> A buggy, the one with the white horse it was. Only Doc Peabody is fat. Three hundred pounds. You ride with him on the uphill side, holding on. Children. Walking easier than holding uphill. *Seen the doctor yet have you seen Caddy*
>
> *I dont have to I cant ask now afterward it will be all right it wont matter*
>
> Because women so delicate so mysterious Father said. Delicate equilibrium of periodical filth between two moons balanced. (147)

The remembered image captures Quentin's and Caddy's anxiety about her suspected pregnancy, about the need to keep it a secret until she is safely married, about Quentin's exclusion from the fundamental mystery of female reproduction. The male view combines exaggerated respect ("so delicate so mysterious") with dread at the "filth" of menstruation (suggested by a phrase later in this passage, "[l]iquid putrefaction") and copulation ("her hips thighs. Outside outside of them always but" [147]). (Quentin projects his repugnance onto the dirty immigrant child, repeatedly referring to her "black" face and once noticing that her hand is "moist and dirty, moist dirt ridged into her flesh" [145].) You feel the tilt of Quentin's whole world in the otherwise puzzling association with Peabody's buggy; Peabody is the Compsons' hometown doctor, so he appears in Quentin's recollection because of Caddy's "medical" problem. But his weight and the funny practice of the children's "holding on" to the uphill side of the vehicle suggest the precarious position of children's well-being in Quentin's memory.

In her blackness and silence, this "sister" represents a Caddy who, in her defilement and absence, shadows Quentin's mind. He can no more restore this child to her home than he can Caddy. At one point he grows desperate in his effort to free himself of the child and return her to her parents: "if you could just slice the walls away all of a sudden Madam, your daughter, if you please. No. Madam, for God's sake, your daughter" (152). And what about father? "your papa's going to be worried about you" (156). Surely the strength of Quentin's anxiety arises from reworking the reactions of his own parents to Caddy's wanderings from home. Under the pressure of his revisionary memory, he fantasizes a correction of the Compsons' indifference to Caddy's behavior. This state of mind leads to the comic conclusion of the episode, when the child's brother recognizes the girl in the company of a stranger. He bolts from his place of work shouting "You steala my seester" (160). This moment so perfectly inverts Quentin's inability to retrieve Caddy that it reduces him to hysterical laughter at his own futility and victimization.

Throughout his last day, Quentin broods on the details of his eventual death by water. Many of the day's events wind around the river far from home that must represent in Quentin's mental map the branch in which he and Caddy played as children. Earlier in the afternoon he has a conversation with several boys who are fishing, and later he and the little girl come across them again, this time as the boys are swimming. Quentin no doubt tests his resolve when he says to his companion: "'Hear them in swimming, sister? I wouldn't mind doing that myself.' If I had time. When I had time. I could hear my watch" (157). Embarrassed, the boys want Quentin and the girl to leave, but Quentin assures them, "She won't hurt you. We just want to watch you for a while" (157). When the boys threaten to "get out and throw them in," Quentin and little sister depart: "That's not for us, is it" (158). Quentin arranges these scenes under the pressure of regret and mourning. As if he could replay their childhood, Quentin longs to remain on the banks of the water, never to let Caddy enter and muddy herself. Like this one, virtually every incident of Quentin's section, as we have seen, directs itself toward denying that the present has turned the past into shadows.

If Caddy has "died" at her lover's touch, is dead to childhood's innocence, and strikes a deathblow to the family name and honor through her shame, then it is only in the shadow of death that Quentin may seek reunion with her. Quentin's suicide—desperate as it is, diseased a solution as we are made to feel it—follows inexorably from his version of the logic of loss. Recalling his classically trained father's remark, but garbling it ironically, Quentin refers to his grandfather's watch as the "reducto absurdum of all human experience" (86). (The actual phrase is "reductio ad absurdum"; it applies to the reduction of an opponent's argument to absurdity.) Though he shields himself from the "blind stupid assertions" of the clock throughout his last day, Quentin only postpones his capitulation to time's reduction of experience to absurdity. Above the waters of the Charles River Quentin stages his final acknowledgment, as well as his final defiance, of the law of loss.

The manner of Quentin's suicide points to the whole network of associations that structure Quentin's mind. His conversation with Mr. Compson suggests that he has decided to arrest time, to halt the process that takes Caddy away from him to begin with and that then goes on to lessen the pain day by day. In the following passage we can see Quentin grapple with the horror that not only love fades, but grief fades as well:

> you are still blind to what is in yourself to that part of general truth the sequence of natural events and their causes which shadows every mans brow even benjys you are not thinking of finitude you are contemplating an apotheosis in which a temporary state of mind will become symmetrical above the flesh and aware both of itself and of the flesh it will not quite discard you will not even be dead and i temporary and he you cannot bear to think that someday it will no longer hurt you like this. (203)

Quentin wants to make his temporary state of mourning permanent ("an apotheosis"); by cutting off his life he can protect his devotion to Caddy from any further erosion.

Second, Quentin dreads the continuation of a life in which nothing happens that has not already happened. The pure power of the past overcomes Quentin. Not only the loss of his beloved sister, but also his familial and cultural belatedness makes him feel as if his life has already ended. Quentin lives out his last day in an echo chamber of remote events, distant voices. We have seen how he wakes up with the thought of his grandfather's watch in his mind and the sound of his father's words in his ear. This son of the South (he never becomes a son of Harvard) cannot escape the conviction that the past is nothing but catastrophe—the catastrophe of the Civil War, slavery, aristocratic decline in the New South, and the humiliation of a ruined family. Like so many other southerners, Quentin sees nothing but a legacy of loss. His suicide suggests that he refuses to accept the repetition of that past in his future. As Mr. Compson says, "was the saddest word of all there is nothing else in the world its not despair until time its not even time until it was" (205). But Quentin amends his father, "Again. Sadder than was. Again. Saddest of all. Again" (109).

After returning from class, Quentin's roommate jokes at finding him dressed in his new suit: "Is it a wedding or a wake?" (93). With awful precision, Shreve's comment points to the final significance of

Quentin's suicide. There is a way in which his taking the plunge resembles a mock marriage ceremony, a wedding-turned-wake. (We might recall how Benjy's memory fuses these two kinds of events; Caddy's wedding and the funerals of Damuddy and Mr. Compson blur in his mind.) So frequently a reflection of Caddy's face appears to Quentin—from the figure running out of the mirror to the face beneath his own as he peers at Caddy lying in the branch. "I ran down the hill in that vacuum of crickets like a breath travelling across a mirror she was lying in the water" (171). The surface of the Charles River becomes the threshold between brother and sister, between self and other. Through it Quentin will crash in a desperate effort to reunite with all he has lost in becoming a separate identity.

The suicide becomes the gesture of narcissistic incest forbidden everywhere but in Quentin's shadowy imagination. It is at once the symbolic loss of virginity and the punishment for doing so through incest; at once the repossession of Caddy and the confession of her utter absence; at once the defiance of his father's belief that no battle is ever even fought and the admission of his defeat; at once the only decisive act of Quentin's life and an act that never takes place in the novel at all. "The peacefullest words. Peacefullest words. *Non fui. Sum. Fui. Non sum.* Somewhere I heard bells once. Mississippi or Massachusetts. I was. I am not" (199).

JASON

Short of actual physical abuse, it would be difficult to imagine an act of greater cruelty to a child than Jason's heartless disposal of his two free show passes in the face of Luster's desperate pleading. Presented late in the section narrated by the middle Compson brother, this scene (292–95) epitomizes Jason's vindictive, resentful, all-devouring malice. For the deprivations, slights, and present burdens he feels, Jason wants others to pay, and pay.

Jason cannot grasp the larger cultural circumstances responsible for much of his suffering, so he strikes out at whoever happens to be handy—his sister, for failing to secure the job promised by her ex-husband; his niece, for scandalizing the family name through her public misbehavior; his mother, for refusing to grant him authority as the head of the house; so all women, for being "bitches"; his father, for squandering the Compson patrimony on a pointless wedding and an equally pointless year's tuition at Harvard; his brother Quentin, for drowning himself and showing the town of Jefferson yet another way in which the Compsons are all crazy; his boss, for treating him like a common employee; blacks, for being lazy and lucky; Jews, Yankees, and New Yorkers for cheating "decent Americans"; his gullible townsmen, for letting themselves be shilled; stupid farmers, for thinking more of an afternoon's diversion than their fields awaiting the plow.

This catalog of Jason's enemies suggests that Faulkner in part wants to explore the psychology of a 1920s southern small-town bigot. Jason's paranoid sense of persecution and the blind hatred it inspires in him surely do add up to the kind of mentality Faulkner knew, sadly, as a type in his world. It is not a long step from Jason's attitudes toward women and blacks to those of Joe Christmas and Percy Grimm in *Light in August* (1932). Christmas, a foundling unsure whether he is white or partly black, kills a philanthropic white woman who was once his lover; and Grimm, seized by hatred for the "rapist"/murderer, hunts him down and executes him brutally. Faulkner shows us how the violence of both actions reveals the intrinsic violence of an unjust society. The New South has not outgrown the legacies of the Old South in which blacks made up the compulsory labor force and white women either worked under the rule of their husbands if they were poor farm people, or idly graced a world of aristocratic leisure if they were well off.

In Faulkner's world, both women and blacks suffer as objects of various sorts of oppression. Poorer white males suffer economically; whites from the aspirant middle class or fallen aristocracy (petit bourgeois is the term traditionally used to describe this class) feel the barriers between them and the status they want; and even the so-called master class of white males become prisoners to strict codes of behavior and prejudice, as well as to the pain of guilt about a history of racial exploitation (though one must say they suffer less than the others).

When I discuss the economic and social background of *The Sound and the Fury*, I will return to the scene in which Jason burns the show tickets. For the moment, however, we can use this scene to isolate Jason's principal obsessions—obsessions that, like his brothers', appear readable under the logic of loss. In part, Jason's cruelty strikes at Dilsey, Luster's grandmother. Though she treats Luster sharply, Dilsey never fails to look after him too; once Jason destroys the passes, she promises to find Luster another quarter to replace the one he has lost earlier (and for which he is looking in the opening pages of the novel). Jason must surely resent the relative warmth of the Gibson family; we recall that Damuddy's death very much aggrieves Jason, the grandson given the privilege of sleeping in her bed and being thought of as belonging to her family, the Bascombs.

Because he is both a black and a child, Luster also represents the spirit of play in a world Jason finds all work. Jason would never go to the show himself; his destruction of the tickets bespeaks a determination to rob Luster of sensual pleasure and idleness. Just as he has whined and tattled, shied away and cried through his own youth, so the adult Jason finds play senseless. He so resents what he sees will be a lifetime of enslavement to a job that he instinctively lashes out at a representative of the black domestics. The servants run the Compson household, indenture Jason as their keeper and find ways to enjoy themselves at his expense.

Finally, Jason also wants revenge on Dilsey. Not only does she oppose him incessantly—insisting that he accommodate his schedule to hers, defending his niece Quentin from his mistreatment, sheltering Benjy from his cruelty—but she also constitutes the feminization of authority that Jason identifies with the South's enfeeblement. His bitter complaints about how free women have become and about his own inability to restore the authority of patriarch that Mr. Compson cynically abdicated reveal Jason's fury at the apparent upheaval of a social order that should be ruled by the force of paternal law. "You've got to learn one thing," he lectures his niece as he squeezes her arm and steals her money, "and that is that when I tell you to do something, you've got it to do" (247). Jason tortures Luster to demonstrate that he remains in charge; no pleading from a child, no reproof from a black servant woman will make him change his mind. Jason's behavior is shocking because it replicates in miniature his culture's tragic foundation on the will to mastery by one race and gender.

Jason's barely restrainable behavior throughout the novel may make us pause over Faulkner's well-known comment in the Compson Appendix (1946) that Jason was the "first sane Compson since before Culloden" (Culloden was a battle fought in 1746 by the Scottish Highlanders against the British; it was disastrous for the Scots). In the long view, Faulkner's remark must be taken ironically; surely Jason borders on paranoia, hysteria, homicidal fury, and suicidal despair. He hardly seems healthier than either of his brothers; rather, the extraordinary beauty and gentleness of Quentin's section make Jason's brutality all the more inhuman, if not insane. Yet in a certain sense Faulkner's notion does accurately indicate the mental processes by which the only genuinely adult Compson brother manages to live out his life. Jason converts his psychic anguish into symbolic embodiments that he can deal with in his everyday reality. To that extent—and Faulkner makes us sense how disquieting this idea is—Jason is quite sane.

Jason's literal preoccupations emerge clearly in his section: he seeks to amass a fortune and he struggles to restore the observance of genteel propriety to the Compson household. Jason wants the Compsons at least to behave as if they were once again one of Jefferson's leading families. Though he possesses a keen sense of the ultimate futility and even macabre comedy of this course of action, Jason pursues it with astonishing devotion. To the very last words of his section he is speaking of a restoration followed by the hope of flight: "I dont want to make a killing; save that to suck in the smart gamblers with. I just want an even chance to get my money back. And once I've done that they can bring all Beale Street and all bedlam in here and two of them can sleep in my bed and another one can have my place at the table too" (305). Jason's longing for restitution corresponds with his brothers' yearning for the recovery of Caddy and what she represents. Everything in Jason's history teaches him that the Compsons are a family of means and pride; he ends up as completely in bondage to that image of an unreal past as are either of his brothers, who have made their memories of Caddy into a fetish. The first step in understanding Jason involves prying below the surface of his furious daily activities and seeing how they serve to cover up Jason's own nostalgia for Caddy.

In a simple way, Jason wants money because it helps soothe other losses. After he cheats Caddy out of the hundred dollars she gives him in exchange for a moment with her daughter, Jason reports, "And so I counted the money again that night and put it away, and I didn't feel so bad. I says I reckon that'll show you. I reckon you'll know now that you cant beat me out of a job and get away with it" (235–36). Stealing Caddy's money partially avenges and compensates Jason, even though he claims that money is essentially meaningless: "After all, like I say money has no value; it's just the way you spend it. It dont belong to anybody, so why try to hoard it. It just belongs to the man that can get it and keep it" (223). Money seems to be one of the few objects in Jason's world that does not carry the taint of association with the emotional history of the Compsons. It is a purely abstract currency to be gained and lost. No social disapproval or stigma attaches to wanting to make money, thus Jason has found a sphere of activity both necessary and respectable.

Yet if we look more closely at the way Jason handles money, we may suspect that his financial scheming subtly translates into economic terms the emotional gains and losses that have formed him. Even in the statement I quoted above, the contradictions in Jason's attitude toward money emerge. If money does not belong to anybody, what does it mean to say that it does belong "to the man that can get it and keep it"? How is keeping money different from hoarding it? Jason hoards the money he embezzles from Caddy—in a strongbox hidden in his closet, no less. These very contradictions correspond with the confusingly self-defeating nature of all of Jason's schemes. Though he knows his New York brokers deceive small country investors like him, Jason cannot bring himself to ignore their advice; if he pays for it, it must be worth something. Though he knows his only escape from the dead ends of the Compson family and the town of Jefferson lies in his interest in Earl's hardware business, he withdraws the principal to buy a car (which, of course, he cannot stand because gasoline makes him sick). Therefore, Jason's financial behavior masks but also indicates unsettled issues in his emotional and psychological bearings.

A first observation about how Jason uses money to conduct psychic business involves the relation he establishes with Caddy. During their childhood, Jason has always been odd man out. In the earlier sections Jason appears as a sulky, selfish loner. As Quentin and Caddy "make interest" with Father against Mrs. Compson in her words (301), Jason lines up as a Bascomb, with his mother, grandmother, and Uncle Maury ("Thank God you are not a Compson, because all I have left now is you and Maury," Mrs. Compson tells him [230]). Ironically, once Jason has assumed responsibility for his niece's upbringing, he is closer to his sister than ever before. Nevertheless, all of their dealings depend on the exchange of money and services, although this produces—in black travesty—the equivalent of parental regard for the female Quentin. Once when they meet to discuss Quentin, Jason notices that he is "feeling [Caddy's] eyes almost like they were touching my face" (241); perhaps he senses what it would have been like to have enjoyed her intimacy in childhood. Such a buried sentiment may also crop up in the following scene, at Mr. Compson's funeral: "We stood there, looking at the grave, and then I got to thinking about when we were little and one thing and another and I got to feeling funny again, kind of mad or something" (233).

Jason's hurt at being spurned by Caddy, Quentin, and Father deepens into fury when the family suffers extreme financial reverses. When, shortly after their marriage, Caddy's husband divorces her after she bears a child that is not his, Jason realizes he has lost the promised position in Herbert Head's bank: "Well," he says when Caddy sends home the infant she cannot afford to keep, "they brought my job home tonight" (227). The "job" grows into Jason's means of exacting harsh retaliation. By intercepting the money sent by Caddy for the child's support, Jason in effect steals back from all the dispossessing women in his life. (Jason's trick involves allowing his mother to destroy, on the grounds of family pride, each of Caddy's monthly checks as they arrive. But Jason provides fake checks for this ceremony, secretly keeping and cashing the authentic ones.) Through these exchanges, Jason seeks to revise the history of his disenfranchisement. He wants literally to restore the patrimony and his own right to it. He wants symbolically to regain power over getting and spending, rights that belong, in his view, to the male heads of families.

Even in his less personal financial dealings, with Wall Street, psychic rather than practical requirements seem to direct Jason's behavior. He wants to win back what he has already lost, but he refuses to change his losing ways. Jason follows the advice of those he knows victimize him and his kind, as if he wants to confirm his analysis of a world in which people must uphold the very rules that do them in, just as Jason turns out to be at once both the greatest casualty and firmest defender of the Compson mentality. He insists on competing as an outsider with "[t]hese damn jews . . . with all their guaranteed inside dope" (270); similarly he has had to compete vainly as an outsider with the inside circle of Caddy, Quentin, Benjy, and Father. He persists in relying on market reports from the town telegraph office, even though they arrive too late to be of any use to him; it is as if he unconsciously acknowledges that time is his enemy as much as it is his brother Quentin's. Jason's activities may be read as a consistent but encoded comment on his family circumstances. Once when he does have to communicate with a family member (to reassure Caddy that her daughter Quentin will write to her), he composes a telegram: "All well. Q writing today." An acquaintance wonders if Jason is signalling his broker: "What are you sending, Jason? . . . Is that a code message to buy?" (221). But we can see that the translation actually runs in the opposite direction—from finance to family matters.

The Compsons' preoccupation with the past (which Faulkner suggests in *Absalom, Absalom!* is typical of the South) ensnares them in patterns of repetition from generation to generation. Jason's efforts to correct his family's decline and his own dispossessions puts him in the ironic position of suffering them all over again. Just as his financial exertions intend to correct both fiscal and psychological losses, so his defense of Compson pride means to redress the blows it has suffered. Desperately wanting to be the sort of strong father Mr. Compson never was, he takes to "fathering" his niece with savage zeal. Watching her every move, Jason tries to make her be respectful, obedient, prompt, dutiful, and chaste—the discipline he thinks his own sister should have gotten. Mrs. Compson appreciates this (even though she also frustrates it), and reminds Quentin that her uncle "is the nearest thing to a father you've ever had" (300).

But correcting the mistakes of one generation is not the only purpose fueling Jason's treatment of Quentin. We also sense that Jason uses Quentin to represent her mother, as if, like the little girl who shadows his brother Quentin, the present might be made to stand for the past. Jason seethes at Caddy through her daughter: "Just like her mother" (245), he fumes after one of her moments of defiance. What Jason considers Quentin's "whoring" reincarnates her mother's, and his devotion to making his niece corrigible springs from his deep resentment of Caddy not only for excluding him—uniquely—from her affections, but also for costing him and his family their financial and social futures.

In the usual swirl of contradiction that engulfs Jason's mind, his niece represents, beyond an object of loathing, an object of longing too. She appeals to him sexually; Jason studies in outraged fascination the way her kimono unwraps around her: "I'll be damned if they dont dress like they were trying to make every man they passed on the street want to reach out and clap his hand on it" (267). Such a gust of interest brings the uncle to the brink of incestuous desire, but Jason stops short of confronting (let alone obeying) that spectre in the Compson history. Yet Jason does seem indirectly preoccupied with incest, the crime that stands—invisibly to his literal-minded eyes—as an emblem of the South's self-love and insistence on marriage strictly within the "family" of whites (see Sundquist [1983] on incest and miscegenation).

Beset by a family in which his mother's loyalty and affection occasion disputes between husband and brother; in which his brother Benjy is a congenital idiot—the popular sign of incest—who was originally named after Uncle Maury, the brother with whom Mrs. Caroline Compson keeps a special Bascomb intimacy; and in which a sister, pregnant, cannot name the father of her own child, but who names that child after her own brother—beset by such a family, it is no wonder that Jason taunts himself with the idea that Caddy and Quentin have actually committed incest. At one point Mrs. Compson complains that her granddaughter must represent a family curse:

> "Sometimes I think she is the judgment of Caddy and Quentin upon me."
> "Good Lord," I says, "You've got a fine mind. No wonder you kept yourself sick all the time."
> "What?" she says. "I don't understand."
> "I hope not," I says. "A good woman misses a lot she's better off without knowing." (301).

Here Jason perversely interprets Mrs. Compson's remark as suggesting a biological likeness between his niece and his sister and brother, Caddy and Quentin. Mrs. Compson surely does not mean this, but Jason uses her incomprehension to measure the limitless contempt he holds for the depravity of his family.

To the extent that Jason's section obeys the logic of loss his brothers' do, his life also embodies the contradictions of repetition as recovery. Just as Benjy and Quentin will be satisfied with nothing except a return to an innocence that perhaps never existed, so Jason uses the means that dispossessed him as the path to restitution. If Caddy has "stolen" his job, he will steal it back in the form of her payments; if the male Compsons, his father and elder brother, have been bettered by women, he will show everyone what being a man means; if the family fortune has bled away through neglect, Jason will conceive the design that will win it all back.

Jason cannot see that the categories responsible for his family's earlier success are beginning to lose their authority. In repeating, or trying to repeat, patterns indebted to a system of supremacy, Jason ends up being victimized by them again. The fullest example of this irony emerges in his niece's theft of the money Jason has hoarded, an episode that carries us into the last section of the novel. Quentin's theft, her running off with the red-tied showman, even her escape from the Compson house by climbing down the pear tree, illustrate that Quentin is a cannier, more threatening version of her mother.

Jason's whole life becomes a desperate repetition of rigid, narrow sets of actions and responses. To be a man in his world, Jason must practice violence and insist on total authority. He warns Quentin, as he fixes to hit her once, that he is "not an old woman, nor an old half dead nigger, either. You damn little slut" (212). Jason's sense of mastery rests on the power vested in white males, yet it is a power that needs to be exercised to be maintained. When Mrs. Compson wonders how modern youngsters can behave so scandalously, Jason points out that "[y]ou had somebody to make you behave yourself./. . . She hasn't" (273). And as much as he resents the degradation of being a wage earner, Jason accepts responsibility for his whole household, his niece included: "I'm a man, I can stand it" (283). Faulkner makes us see the pity of Jason's imprisonment in a code of behavior that destroys both master and victim, white and black, man and woman. The Jason Compson who spends his whole life trying to right his world after recent family events have upset it ends up realizing that the sins of one generation have carried over and covered those of the next. Yet another "promiscuous" female Compson has disappeared with the family fortune into the arms of a lover: like mother, like daughter. Jason fails to see that every effort to reimpose an unjust order generates the conditions for its overthrow.

Jason does realize that his world has lost the coherence he believes it once must have possessed. As we will discuss more fully in the next chapter, the contradictions of southern culture emerge in this historical period of transition as the Old South, still venerated during the period of Yankee occupation and Reconstruction, gives way to the so-called New South. At such turnings, cultures often exhibit stress lines, points at which their values are subjected to pressure. Jason plays these contradictions out in a particularly acute way, both in his behavior, as we have seen, and in some of the more puzzling pronouncements of the last Compson.

Jason's preoccupations as he experiences them are illustrated in Jason's remarks on gender and family. We have seen that Jason's world identifies force with masculine authority, yet his section repeatedly demonstrates the impotence of such a set of values in the moment of crisis. "Do you think I need any man's help to stand on my feet?" Jason asks of his mother in rejecting Caddy's money, "Let alone a woman that cant name the father of her own child?" (303). Yet for all his protestation of manliness, Jason covertly acknowledges that women hold the (phallic) power in his world. His niece, for example, so "unmans" him by her defiance and boldness that he fantasizes incoherently about her need to be "castrated": "I says I know what you need, you need what they did to Ben then you'd behave" (292).

Jason's treatment of his female companion Lorraine reflects a similar anxiety about his manhood. It is typical of him that he should try to convince us that violence is the secret of his mastery of women: "Always keep them guessing. If you cant think of any other way to surprise them, give them a bust in the jaw" (222). But when Jason imagines Lorraine boasting to the other prostitutes about him, plenty of doubt colors his fantasy: "Lorraine telling them he may not drink but if you dont believe he's a man I can tell you how to find out she says If I catch you fooling with any of these whores you know what I'll do she says" (269). Yearning for Lorraine's consolation after his money has been stolen, Jason seems more the little boy at his mother's breast than the virile lover: "He imagined himself in bed with her, only he was just lying beside her, pleading with her to help him, then he thought of the money again, and that he had been outwitted by a woman, a girl" (355). The crisis of authority besetting the Compsons, and the entire New South that they represent, provides the eroding foundation for Jason's fury. The more he insists on the old, "right" way of doing things, the more we may be sure those ways have lost their potency if not their appeal to some.

In the closing passage of the section, from which I quoted earlier, we notice how Jason cannot separate his dream of final victory over past dispossessions from repudiating the very table he will finally, rightfully master: "I just want an even chance to get my money back. And once I've done that they can bring all Beale Street and all bedlam in here and two of them can sleep in my bed and another one can have my place at the table too" (305). Here the would-be head of the family abdicates at the moment of recovery, as if gesturing toward the obsolescence of the very forms he insists upon upholding.

If time is the universal conceptualization of concrete change, Quentin's obsession with timepieces, previously discussed, indicates the way he abstracts the force that victimizes him. Quentin considers time his enemy, but in so doing he ignores another, more immediate temporal process: history. By mistaking mere clock time as the problem, Quentin dodges the historical conditions that have contributed to his overvaluation of virginity, incest, purity, changelessness. When he explores the South's history in *Absalom, Absalom!*, Quentin will come to grasp the relation between universal temporality—time—and one's personal and regional history—the concrete events, attitudes, and social arrangements that shape individual experience. Jason proves to be Quentin's brother as he wages his own battle with time.

In Jason's case, time becomes further reduced to matters of the clock. Jason spends his days rushing from one self-imposed task to the next, fuming continually over his shortage of time: "I went back to the store. It was half past three almost. Damn little time to do anything in, but then I am used to that. I never had to go to Harvard to learn that" (270–71). Time is leisure to Jason, and he has none: "I never had time to go to Harvard like Quentin or drink myself into the ground like Father. I had to work" (207). Time is also money to Jason, and he does not have enough: Caddy offers him a hundred dollars to see her child, and Jason—with literal-minded cruelty—gives her her "minute" in exchange (233–36). Even Jason's strange joke about how his boss monitors his absences points to this relation between time and money: "'You ought to have a dollar watch,' I says. 'It wont cost you so much to believe it's lying each time'" (283).

These remarks, like Jason's obsession with getting the household to run on time and making his niece prompt, indicate Jason's efforts to restrict the effects of time. If he can insist on his authority over his own day, over his household's schedule, over Quentin's tardiness, over the investments that turn time into appreciation rather than loss, then Jason believes he will have mastered time, the condition of life that Mr. Compson says "shadows every mans brow even benjys." The irony of Jason's life springs from his incapacity to see that the clock has little to do with history and that the South in which he has grown up has lost its authority to order life.

"Once a bitch always a bitch, *what I say*" (206, emphasis added). From the notoriously hateful line that begins his section, we listen to Jason pride himself on his power of assertion. He spouts opinions he takes to be entirely his own, and the more extravagantly incomprehensible the opinions the more original he believes them to be. Jason surprises his cronies, for instance, by saying he does not believe Babe Ruth's 1928 Yankees can win the pennant because they are "shot" and no team "can be that lucky forever" (291). (The 1927 Yankees were one of the most overpowering teams in the history of baseball. The team that featured the famed "Murderers' Row" of hitters was anchored by Babe Ruth, and—heedless of Jason's prediction—they won another World Championship in 1928.) Besides suggesting that Jason will never bet on a sure thing because he is so in love with losing, his opinions about baseball also indicate how deeply his southern mentality is ingrained in him. No one who rails as wildly as Jason does against New York brokers and "Yankee" exploitation could root for the team from the hub of northern financial domination. This Jason Lycurgus Compson—now the fourth in his family—proves to be not so "different [a] breed of cat from Father" (231) after all. Faulkner shows us the relentless, pervasive power of the South's

history to condition the most personal of attitudes. Though his brother Quentin awakens with what "Father said" in his overwhelmed
eaar Jason is no less "spoken" by his family and culture. The most
vicious expressions of mastery, brutalization, and violence originate
not in Jason himself, but in the social realities that speak through
him. He is never less in control of his speech than when he says "I
say."

•   •   •

As Faulkner turns his novel away from utterances by individual
characters after the first three sections, he begins to weigh more fully
the effects of race, gender, and region on the telling of the Compson
story. Though the idea for the novel began with the image of Caddy
climbing the pear tree to peer into the room where Damuddy's funeral
is taking place, and though the initial spheres of interest in the novel
have to do with the emotional, intellectual, and psychological consequences of that loss on each of the three Compson brothers, by the
last section of the novel Faulkner has opened his focus to consider
how this world will look to an outsider (including the reader), and
how even an apparently objective third-person narrative reveals a social and historical identity as pronounced as each of the Compson
brothers'.

"FAULKNER"

In entitling each section of my interpretation according to the name
of its narrator, I have followed a practice common to virtually all critics of the novel. Scholars traditionally refer to Benjy's section, not to
"April Seventh, 1928." Most readers find this method preferable because it identifies each unit of narrative by its outstanding characteristic, its narrator. Even careful readers may not remember exactly
which date of the April weekend belongs to which section, but no one
can forget that the opening ninety pages of *The Sound and the Fury*
never leave the mind of an idiot. Moreover, a later work by Faulkner
encourages this practice; in *As I Lay Dying* (1930), fifteen narrators

collaborate on the story, and each of the fifty-nine separate sections appears under the heading or title of one of their names. Unmistakably, Faulkner associates each narrative point of view with an individual identity.

In the case of the last section of *The Sound and the Fury*, however, we may be led astray by the urge to attribute the narrative to a character. Because the preceding three sections are first-person narratives, both the speaker and principal subject may be represented by a single name. Benjy's section is his because he is at once the narrator and the narrated; we listen to him as he reports what happens to him. But the last section has no identifiable narrator. The narrative is not produced by a voice speaking in the first person (no "I" addresses us). Most readers do agree, however, that Dilsey Gibson serves as the focus of attention for much of the section, so critics have gotten into the habit of referring to "April Eighth, 1928" as Dilsey's section. (*The Portable Faulkner* reprinted this section under the heading "Dilsey.") I believe this custom glosses over a problem that Faulkner wants to keep before us; through Dilsey's point of view, but not in her own words, the reader acquires a new perspective on the Compson family troubles. Dilsey's lack of a voice to call her own tells us a great deal about which race and gender hold the authority to speak in Faulkner's world.

One of the reasons for *The Sound and the Fury*'s status as a great novel involves this intersection of formal and thematic sophistication. On the one hand, Faulkner experiments as an artist with the purely formal aspects of his craft. Like the postimpressionist and cubist painters whose work he saw and admired during his stay in Paris during 1925, Faulkner the modernist takes apart the conventional sequential narrative. He tries to render the same subject from a variety of angles, telling the "same" story from several narrative viewpoints. He dispenses with the strict observance of linear chronology, breaking time into units that he arranges according to psychological or emotional prominence, as we have seen, rather than according to how events happen to occur. Even at the level of style, as we recall from our discussion of Quentin's section especially, Faulkner upends the conventions of realistic prose and represents Quentin's mind as a swirl of images, sensations, half-sentence recollections, broken thoughts.

By the time we arrive at the last section of the novel we can appreciate an important effect of our reading experience: no story is ever exempt from the conditions that produce it. No narrative—no matter how impersonal and objective—ever manages to escape the set of cultural assumptions from which it takes its viewpoint, just as each of the first three sections have shown how certain personal and social preoccupations saturate each narrator and condition the story each can tell. In describing how he composed *The Sound and the Fury,* Faulkner points to this effect by naming the last narrator "Faulkner," as if this speaker carries no more authority than any of the other characters/narrators and is no more successful than they in communicating the whole story: "It was, I thought, a short story, something that could be done in about two pages, a thousand words, I found out it couldn't. I finished it the first time, and it wasn't right, so I wrote it again, and that was Quentin, that wasn't right. I wrote it again, that was Jason, that wasn't right, then I tried to let Faulkner do it, that still was wrong" (*University,* 32).

In effect, Faulkner's narrative experimentation has broken down the distinction between first- and third-person narrative. All narrative must be read as coming from a source that is at once personal (in the sense that someone is, as it were, producing the words as an act of communication) and impersonal (in the sense that every utterance depends on some sort of collectively recognized codes to make its meaning intelligible to others). Thoreau makes much the same point on the opening page of *Walden,* his fictionalized autobiographical account of his two years' sojourn at Walden Pond: "In most books, the *I,* or first person, is omitted; in this it will be retained; that, in respect to egotism, is the main difference. We commonly do not remember that it is, after all, always the first person that is speaking."

Although the last section appears to be straightforwardly objective third-person narrative, our experience of reading the earlier sections should prepare us for assessing the narrator's confinement to particular circumstances and ways of seeing and saying. Like Thoreau, Faulkner wants us to remember that it is always the first person that is speaking. To do so in the world of *The Sound and the Fury* is to recollect that the narrator remains outside some of the characters and experiences he would describe. The last section tensely opposes "Faulkner"'s narration and Dilsey's point of view. The novel's experimentalism is wed to the most serious inquiry into the social reality of the South in 1928. The result is a work that vigorously considers the relation between how reality is represented and who is doing the representation.

The narrator assumes greater authority over his narrative than his predecessors have. From the opening sentence—"The day dawned bleak and chill" (306)—the reader enjoys an expanded focus and descriptive register. As in a more traditional realistic novel, the narrator attempts to fill in the world the characters inhabit, to convey the atmosphere of their place and time, to present their appearance and behavior. For the first time in the novel, someone tries to make us touch and see the world of the characters from the outside. We may feel the dustlike rain that coats Dilsey's skin as she stands outside her door looking at a rainy Easter Sunday morning (the mist "a substance partaking of the quality of thin, not quite congealed oil" [306]). We may envision how the "weathered church lifted its crazy steeple like a painted church, and the whole scene was flat and without perspective as a painted cardboard set upon the ultimate edge of the flat earth" (337). We may startle at the sudden visibility of characters' faces: Jason, "with close-thatched brown hair curled into two stubborn hooks, one on either side of his forehead like a bartender in caricature"; Caroline, "with perfectly white hair and eyes pouched and baffled and so dark as to appear to be all pupil or all iris (323)"; and Benjy, with "skin dead looking and hairless; dropsical too, he moved with a shambling gait like a trained bear" (317).

Earlier sections have not failed to give us sensual images, but the final section aspires to a more authoritatively comprehensive and objective account. The narrator's exterior descriptions conform to the more familiar codes by which we order and categorize our perceptions and by which realistic fiction portrays reality. We may sense a corresponding move in the novel toward summing up, and toward making meaning more explicit.

Notice the way the narrator spells out more universal meanings for features of the Compson world. Benjy's howling represents "all time and injustice and sorrow become vocal for an instant" (333). The narrator interprets other symbols as well: to Jason, Quentin has become "the very symbol of the lost job itself" (355). Clever readers already may have figured out why the golfers so upset Benjy, but in the last pages Faulkner finally gives us both pieces of the Caddy/caddie pun: " 'Here, caddie. Bring the bag.' . . . Ben went on at his shambling trot, clinging to the fence. . . . 'All right, den' Luster said, 'You want somethin to beller about?' . . . 'Caddy! Beller now. Caddy! Caddy! Caddy!' " (365).

The narrator seems to want the meaning of images and events to be more clearly resolved in the final section, as if realizing that he has only one more opportunity to succeed before the novel draws to a close. However it simplifies the actual process of composition, Faulkner's story about writing the novel once, realizing it was not "right," writing it again, and so on until "Faulkner" had the last chance, which still was not right, does suggest the open-ended quality of *The Sound and the Fury*. Like many modernist works, *The Sound and the Fury* deliberately organizes itself as a series of fragments. To the extent that modernist forms in the arts mean to reflect a generation's belief that moral, aesthetic, and social coherence have disintegrated, *The Sound and the Fury* can be viewed as Faulkner's most distinctly modernist novel (see Kartiganer 1979). Yet against the sense that the novel is doomed to repeat the Compson story over and over, against Quentin's despairing "If things just finished themselves" (90), against the vision of Jason's "invisible life ravelled out about him like a wornout sock" (362), the novel makes an effort to draw conclusions, settle meaning, and provide the sense of an ending.

The very mood of conclusion colors the final section. Time seems to have finally rung out the Compsons: "The clock tick-tocked solemn and profound. It might have been the dry pulse of the decaying house itself" (329). The members of the House of Compson sense their doom as well: Jason "for the first time . . . saw clear and unshadowed the disaster toward which he rushed" (358); he thinks that "this is how it'll end, and he believed that he was about to die" (359); even Mrs. Compson, beset by hints of another Compson generation's predisposition to scandal and possibly even suicide (she thinks her granddaughter has killed herself when she is discovered missing), "when faced at last by the incontrovertible disaster . . . exhumed from somewhere a sort of fortitude, strength" (346).

Dilsey's memorable reaction to the sermon she has heard, "I seed de beginnin, en now I sees de endin" (344), crystallizes this longing for conclusion. As they end, novels tend to gather themselves up, to dispose of characters, resolve plots, put everything—as the last words of *The Sound and the Fury* have it—"each in its ordered place" (371). Readers may naturally expect novels, if not our lives, to possess shape and coherence. How does Rev. Shegog's sermon prompt Dilsey to envision the shape that explains her life and those of her two families?

We learn that Dilsey's "negro" church has invited a guest speaker for their Easter Sunday service. Brought all the way from Saint Louis, the tiny visitor who follows their own imposing pastor to the platform fails to impress the congregation. Yet Shegog's performance achieves several sublime moments and produces Dilsey's tearful rapture at its conclusion. Shegog chooses to organize his resurrection sermon around the refrain, "I got the recollection and the blood of the Lamb!" (Later, when he modulates from his "white man"'s voice into black dialect, this is rendered as, "I got de ricklickshun en de blood of de Lamb!") The sermon celebrates Christ's sacrificial death at Calvary, his burial, and resurrection on the third day. The congregation joins Shegog in ritually recollecting this event, and in so doing they practice the age-old Christian custom of reaffirming the regenerative power of Christ's sacrifice. For Baptists like the Gibsons, every believer appropriates Christ's death as his or her own (enduring the Father's punishment for human sinfulness), and then partakes of Christ's triumph over death figured in his resurrection. "As in Adam all died, so in Christ shall all be made alive." "Dey kilt Me dat ye shall live again; I died dat dem whut sees en believes shall never die" (343). The act of identification with Christ's suffering and redemption constitutes the believer's faith and assures him or her an eternal place in heaven.

Dilsey surely trusts this interpretation of mortal existence. By grasping the suffering of Christ and his heartbroken mother ("We gwine to kill yo little Jesus!" [342]), Dilsey can glimpse the master analogy for her own suffering. As she ministers to the abusive Mrs. Compson, outwits and defuses the cruel Jason, shelters the innocent child Benjy, she martyrs herself after the model of Christ. "You's de Lawd's chile, anyway," she reassures Benjy, "En I be His'n too, fo long, praise Jesus" (367). Dilsey's vision of the beginning and the ending lifts her experience entirely out of earthly time—out of the suffering of her own life of bondage to the Compsons, out of the history that has determined the fate of her race, class, and gender. Dilsey's faith consoles her with the promise of life beyond time, beyond history.

Such a solution to her otherwise intolerable lot allows Dilsey to live her life tranquilly and authoritatively. Her particular strain of southern Protestantism preached social quiescence. Largely inculcated by slaveowners into their unruly and "uncivilized" blacks throughout the antebellum South, this version of Christianity aimed to justify the political and racial privilege of the master class by rationalizing it as religious responsibility. White slave lords had to look out for the spiritual welfare of their slaves' untutored "savage" souls; they did so by emphasizing the Scriptures' respect for given political and social institutions, by teasing out interpretations of isolated biblical passages that hinted at the racial inferiority of dark peoples, and by devaluing mere earthly life in the face of eternity's rich compensations (see Genovese 1972).

Guided by the precepts of this religious heritage, Dilsey leads her life as if it were something she must endure to finally begin her real

life with Jesus above. Perhaps the most telling indication of her attitude emerges in her accommodation of time. Unlike Quentin and
Jason, Dilsey remains at peace with the clock. She quietly conforms to
its rule and even corrects it when it misspeaks: "On the wall above a
cupboard, invisible save at night, by lamp light and even then evincing
an enigmatic profundity because it had but one hand, a cabinet clock
ticked, then with a preliminary sound as if it had cleared its throat,
struck five times. / 'Eight oclock,' Dilsey said" (316–17). As she goes
about her chores and sees to others' needs, Dilsey can serenely sing to
herself ("something without particular tune or words, repetitive,
mournful and plaintive, austere" [312]) because her life has already
been lived, her suffering has already been redeemed by the recollection
and the blood of the Lamb.

Bands of Christian believers have regularly practiced the ritual of
the Eucharist, the sharing of bread and wine in symbolic celebration
of Christ's broken body and shed blood. Jesus established this sacra-
ment at the Last Supper with his disciples. Though Dilsey's congregation does not literally celebrate the Eucharist, or communion,
during this service, its effect can be seen in the moment of fusion they
enjoy. As Shegog speaks, "the congregation seemed to watch with its
own eyes while the voice consumed him, until he was nothing and
they were nothing and there was not even a voice but instead their
hearts were speaking to one another in chanting measures beyond the
need for words" (340).

But the theology of Dilsey's vision accounts for only part of this
moment's prominence in *The Sound and the Fury*. Shegog's sermon
also binds together the congregation as a black community. The loss
of self into community occurs only when Shegog drops his educated
style and readdresses the congregation in his and their own dialect:
"They did not mark just when his intonation, his pronunciation, became negroid, they just sat swaying a little in their seats as the voice
took them into itself" (341). I want to stress that the sermon reaffirms
the solidarity of the black community in the face of ever present
oppression from without. Shegog's "negroid" voice is entitled to point
to the persecutions of the Israelites in Egyptian bondage, for example,

because, like those other enslaved people, southern blacks saw them-selves as a nation awaiting deliverance. (The black spiritual "Go Down Moses" exemplifies the pervasive analogy slaves drew between the Israelites and themselves; and Faulkner uses the song's title for his 1942 novel about the continued legacy of racial inequality and exploitation.)

The harsh behavior of "de Roman police," Mary's fright at the threat of "de sojer face" who's "gwine to kill yo little Jesus," the prom-ise of real justice when "de doom crack en [I] hears de golden horns shoutin down de glory" (342–43) all point to specific reassurances for blacks in a hostile white society. Shegog reminds them that they are "breddren en sisthun," a family, a social entity that, collectively, can stand unto itself. Walking home, Dilsey warns Frony, "You tend to yo business en let de white folks tend to deir'n" (344). One of the most satisfying ironies of southern history arises from the way slaves found in their masters' Christianity the promises of eventual freedom, justice, and equality that stiffened their resistance to continued brutalization and oppression (Genovese 1972). The last section takes place on 8 April, which was indeed Easter Sunday in 1928; but the next day, 9 April, marks the anniversary of Lee's surrender to Grant at Appo-mattox in 1865, the "ending" of slavery and the "beginning" of free-dom.

Finally, Rev. Shegog's sermon also brings us back to an aspect of *The Sound and the Fury* we have noticed before—the novel's intense self-awareness of the very processes of narrative art. If we consider for a moment that the sermon episode involves an act of the profoundest communication between speaker and hearers, we can appreciate how Faulkner may be exploring the essential nature of verbal performance through this scene. The sermon succeeds in transmitting the preacher's vision to his audience. As Shegog rolls through all that he "sees"—"de blastin, blindin sight" of the whole passion of Christ, from his ar-rest through his resurrection—the congregation too begins to see: "Mmmmmmmmmmmmm. Jesus! I sees, O Jesus!" sings out a listener (343). Dilsey's last word at this moment confirms its achievement: "'He seed de power en de glory.' 'Yes, suh. He seed hit. Face to face he seed hit.' . . . 'I've seed de first en de last'" (344). In the sermon's urgent eloquence, in its willingness to search for the right words for its audience, in its engulfment of speaker and listener in the presence of voice, in its transformation of sound into image, the sermon represents in one way a writer's highest ambition.

By coming at this precise moment in the novel, moreover, the sermon offers an "orthodox" myth that explains the broadest historical realities of the South, the mutual legacies of black suffering, white exploitation, and cultural collapse that are represented in the entwined stories of the Compsons and the Gibsons. The fall from innocence into historical knowledge suggested by Quentin's misery, Jason's ferocious efforts to preserve a social system in ruins, Caddy's and her daughter's flagrant defiance of that system, Dilsey's quiet determination to subvert its authority even as she works within it—all these may be explained by the pattern of Edenic sin, the exile from the garden, the descent into labor, property, and domination, and the ultimate divine redemption of human failure. Spanned across the Easter weekend, the expiration of the Compson house may be read in this mythic framework. It is as if Shegog's sermon also represents the author's wish to see genuine coherence and significance emerge from this chronicle of his region's decline and fall.

Yet the effort to place the novel's materials conclusively "each in its ordered place" does not finally hold. The vision that would explain all immediately grows inaccessible; the plot lines that might conclude with Dilsey's sense of a true "endin" to the "Compson devilment" stray off inconclusively; and the hope of eternal justification and divine justice gets lost amid the reimposition of earthly inequality. We might notice first that Dilsey cannot (or will not) explain her vision even to her family. When Frony asks her "First en last whut?" she responds, "Never you mind" (344). As in the earlier sections of the novel, the solitude of the individual outlook reasserts itself; because Dilsey's summing up remains hers alone, we return to a world that lacks social and familial unity.

If Dilsey reminds Frony that blacks and whites do not have the same "business" in the South, and if she cannot communicate her explanatory vision even to her daughter, we should not be surprised that the narrator "Faulkner" remains substantially outside the lives of characters like the Gibsons. I will develop this point from another angle when we discuss the themes of race and gender in *The Sound and the Fury*, but for the moment notice how the narrator's description of the sermon scene distances him and us from the event the participants experience. Because the tiny black preacher unlooses a huge white voice at them, the congregation "listened at first through curiosity, as they would have to a monkey talking" (339). The comparison indicates the viewpoint of a detached, white narrator, not that of the congregation. Likewise, as Dilsey leads Benjy toward the church, the narrator notices that trees lining the road seemed "to feed upon the rich and unmistakable smell of negroes in which they grew" (336), and that the blacks "looked at Ben with the covertness of nocturnal animals" (337). At moments like these, and there are many of them in the last section, I think Faulkner means to show that even his "own" effort at third-person, objective narration inevitably is colored by the legacies of racism, classism, and sexism. The narrator cannot help but speak from the position of a literate white southern male. Though no individual can wholly escape the circumstances that shape his or her way of sorting and naming the world, great works of art can help us confront the consequences of such prejudices.

After the church service, the novel trails off in a number of directions. The Gibsons return home to renewed squabbling and the crisis of Quentin's disappearance with Jason's money. Jason sets out in pursuit of his niece, but fails to enlist the aid of the sheriff. Blinded by rage into attacking one of the circus people, he is further humiliated by an assault he cannot ward off, a wound he cannot repay, and payment to a common black for the service of driving him from Mottson back to Jefferson. The last scene of the novel pictures him taking his rage out on the insubordinate Luster, who has driven Benjy in reverse direction around the town square and set his charge howling in protest at this violation of routine. Jason's mortification that such a public spectacle should remind the town of how the Compsons have become a "laughing stock" (351) provokes his anger; he wants, in more ways than he can know, for everything to be returned to "its ordered place." Yet the novel suggests that the fates of blacks, women, and the white male ruling class still remain unresolved; symbolized by the fugitive Quentin, the forces of upheaval remain at large.

The Chandler house in Oxford, Mississippi, a few blocks from Faulkner's childhood home. Faulkner's first-grade teacher and her family, including a mentally retarded brother, lived here. An iron fence bordered the front lawn.

Yet Caddy's open efforts to escape the prison of others' expectations do register the discontentment of those who do not have majority voices in the New South. Besides her trips up and down the pear tree outside her window—defiantly to look at death, defiantly to join her lovers—Caddy also speaks her protest. When Jason goes too far and tricks her out of the hundred dollars she pays to see her infant daughter for "a minute," she shows up in Jason's place of business: "'Liar,' she says, 'Liar.' / 'Are you crazy?' I says. 'What do you mean? coming in here like this?' She started in, but I shut her off. I says, 'You already cost me one job; do you want me to lose this one too? If you've got anything to say to me, I'll meet you somewhere after dark'" (236). Jason seeks to silence the voice of female complaint, to banish it from daylight and the world of business activity. But Caddy's "liar" at least briefly names the deceitfulness upon which the society disenfranchises some of its members.

If Caddy calls "liar," her daughter cries "thief." In important respects Quentin furthers Caddy's rebellion against masculine authority. She too climbs in and out of her bedroom in defiance of family authority and social propriety. Yet she has moved beyond Caddy in having no maternal inclination (she does nothing for Benjy that might remind us of her mother's tenderness toward him); instead, her truculence and rage brew until she finds a way to gain her revenge. In her theft of Jason's secret hoard, the money he has been stealing from Caddy and indirectly from his mother, Quentin repeats and nullifies Jason's own vengefulness, thereby using a weapon of the patriarchy against itself. To Caddy's protofeminist defiance of petit bourgeois morality, Quentin adds another charge: when Jason tries to get her to believe that her mother has sent only ten dollars to her, Quentin replies, "'You're lying,' she says. 'Thief!' she says, 'Thief!'" (245). Like blacks, women have had the authority over their economic and moral fates taken from them.

Indeed, as I will point out shortly, in Jason's version of the New South the designation "nigger" refers as much to economic and moral station as to biological race. "When people act like niggers," he explains his niece's misbehavior to his mother, "no matter who they are the only thing to do is treat them like a nigger" (208). Faulkner uses a very interesting vocabulary to describe Quentin's insubordination. Noticing that his niece has dressed provocatively for school and seems to be missing her classes, Jason confronts her: "I want to know what you mean, playing out of school and telling your grandmother lies and forging her name on your report and worrying her sick. What do you mean by it?" (211). What women like Quentin mean by such behavior is to resist domination. Quentin's "playing out," telling "lies," and "forging" suggest her capacity to imagine subversion, to frame acts that challenge and appropriate the authority of those who are dedicated to silencing and controlling her. Like a sister of Huck Finn, she decides that if her uncle represents civilization, she would be better off elsewhere: "'I dont care,' she says, 'I'm bad and I'm going to hell, and I dont care. I'd rather be in hell than anywhere where you are'" (217).

Once Quentin has run off, we see her bedroom through the eyes of her oppressors, Mrs. Compson and Jason, and her defender, Dilsey. Not only does the room suggest the persistence of female victimization (since it has been her mother's room), but it also shows that society gives Quentin limited means for expressing her genuine self: "It was not a girl's room. It was not anybody's room, and the faint scent of cheap cosmetics and the few feminine objects and the other evidences of crude and hopeless efforts to feminize it but added to its anonymity, giving it that dead and stereotyped transience of rooms in assignation houses" (326). This chamber represents the confinement of the female. It it not a room of Quentin's own; she occupies it as if it were another's, or, more accurately, no one's. That dissociation is part of the strength of her independence. So the narrator of the final section looks in vain for the authentically "feminine" signs that would identify the room as hers, failing to appreciate that such touches would signal only the prisoner's acceptance of imprisonment. That the room suggests Quentin's promiscuity to the narrator ("assignation houses") lets us see that Quentin, like her mother, is driven to rebel against her community's values by, tragically, degrading herself all the more, at least in the narrator's eyes. Yet the novel may invite us to see beyond that view—perhaps Quentin's resistance commands our respect to the extent that she experiences her behavior as opening up the means of pleasure and escape otherwise forbidden to her. The narrator's description of Quentin's tragedy rests on heavily patriarchal values upholding "stereotyped" femininity and purity.

Jason's cruelty magnifies the assumptions of patriarchal social systems. Faulkner uses him to focus on the enormous urge to maintain power at the expense of those forced to remain dependent, and to reveal the fundamental contradictions of the social forms that preserve white male domination. Seeing the various kinds of noncooperation on the part of the women in *The Sound and the Fury* as forms of protest might enable us to appreciate the novel's questioning of the world the Compson males wish would return. Certainly such a reading helps to make even unsympathetic characters like Mrs. Compson more understandable.

Mrs. Compson seems a staunch supporter of the head of the household's authority. She reminds her granddaughter that they both owe Jason their obedience because "It's his bread you and I eat" (300). Elsewhere she upholds the code of aristocratic pride (claiming that her family, the Bascombs, are the equal of the Compsons) and insisting that her family observe the proprieties of their station (such as not using nicknames). She is conventionally ambitious for her children; it is "Mother's dream" that Quentin go to Harvard, and Mrs. Compson whisks Caddy off to the resort at French Lick (in Indiana) in the summer of 1909 to find a suitably wealthy husband.

In her reactions to the misfortunes of the family, Mrs. Compson seems equally conventional, although a touch excessive. Caddy's earliest sexual escapade, when she is caught kissing one of the town boys, plunges her mother into theatrical dismay: she dons "a black dress and veil . . . saying her little daughter was dead" (264). When Caddy disgraces the family by being divorced by her husband, Mrs. Compson prohibits her daughter's name from being spoken. She cuts off all communication with her fallen daughter, going so far as destroying the checks sent for the upkeep of Caddy's abandoned daughter. "If she could grow up never to know that she had a mother, I would thank God" (229), Mrs. Compson says to her husband. As the family's predicament worsens, Mrs. Compson falls further and further into hypochondriacal retreat: "Thank God I dont know about such wickedness. I dont even want to know about it. I'm not like most people" (299).

When we see how indifferent Mrs. Compson is to any but her own comparatively light suffering, and think of her ingratitude for Dilsey's service, we may be tempted to dismiss her as a caricature of feeble aristocratic pretension. Such an interpretation cannot be denied, and yet we may also appreciate the restrictions that beset Mrs. Compson as sharply as any other woman in the novel. Throughout her life Caroline Compson has abided by the standards of her society. To have any identity in her world as a woman, she has had to subscribe to the code defining what it means to be a "lady." From virginal youth, through a marriage proper to her station, to the reproduction of the male lineage (the new Quentins and Jasons to replace those of earlier generations), Mrs. Compson has accepted the strict alternatives of her milieu: "I was taught that there is no halfway ground that a woman is either a lady or not" (118).

We may read Mrs. Compson's coldness and hypochondria as defenses and protests. If the passage from virgin to mother is not trouble-free for all females, perhaps Mrs. Compson's refusal to mother her children after bearing them signals a problem with the code rather than the individual governed by it. Perhaps Mrs. Compson's abnormal overvaluation of virginity for her daughter Caddy unconsciously expresses her own discontentment with the narrow categories society allowed women. Perhaps Mrs. Compson is acting as if she remained the secluded virgin rather than the available mother; thus her behavior indicates the internal contradiction behind the virginal mother/maternal virgin ideology of the southern lady (see Weinstein 1989 and Seidel 1985). And might not Mrs. Compson's feigned illnesses be an unconscious parody of the helplessness, immobility, and absence of desire that the patriarchy demands of its women and that we have seen Caddy rebel against more openly? Caddy's and her mother's antagonism conceals their profoundly kindred suffering.

•   •   •

Seen from the later standpoints of *Absalom, Absalom!* (1936) or the Compson Appendix (1946), *The Sound and the Fury* appears to offer a case study of the breakup of the southern rural aristocracy, a late but accurate example of the replacement of the agrarian economy by mercantile capitalism. It places the date of the Old South's termination somewhere around 1910, the date C. Vann Woodward (1957) names for the inception of the New South. Quentin's suicide in 1910 on the eve of Confederacy Memorial Day (celebrated on 3 June by many southern states because it was Jefferson Davis's birthday) seems to put the ideals of the Old South to rest. By the end of the decade following World War I, Jason Compson IV has firmly if madly accommodated himself to the new ways. (We know that Jason becomes a successful merchant in the New South from what Faulkner says about him in the Compson Appendix.) Indeed, the contour of this evolution accords perfectly with Woodward's account of the formation of the New South.

The Sound and the Fury reflects the way in which the emergence of the New South created a nostalgically fictional version of the Old South that could thus be both honored and replaced. Not until after Reconstruction, when the lessons of northern industrial entrepreneurship were embraced by the chastened and newly ambitious South, did the cult of antebellum splendor really take hold. The novel suggests that at the moment of most severe crisis for the survival of the dominant class and its ideology, that ideology's contradictions surface in the very process of reconsolidating itself. What seems to be the simple passage from old to new in *The Sound and the Fury* turns out to be the disguised, partial reinvigoration of the dominant ideology. The mercantile capitalism of the New South obscures its affinity with the agrarian, slaveholding capitalism of the Old South precisely because it rests on the same foundation of economic and racial exploitation. Thus the cult of nostalgia for the Old South accomplishes two purposes: on the one hand, it seems to acknowledge that the days of plantation mentality are a thing of the past, nothing but the stuff of magnolias-and-crinoline historical romances; on the other, it betrays a deeper recognition that the New South is built on the very assumptions of privilege by class, race, and property that organized the slaveholding South. Though there may be new residents in the upper tiers of southern aristocracy, the notion of a white, leisured, monied class who control the means of agricultural and industrial production remains unchanged.

At the point in modern southern history at which a family like the Compsons (or the Falkners) appears to have finally lost its economic privilege and social prestige altogether, the future may loom as a total overthrowing of the past. Benjy's section voices this dread in an early exchange between Mrs. Compson and her servants. Worrying about the plans for an expedition to the cemetery, Mrs. Compson complains that the more sedate Roskus is unavailable to drive the family: "It seems to me you all could furnish me with a driver for the carriage once a week. It's little enough I ask" (10). Dilsey has already observed that the decrepit vehicle is "going to fall to pieces under you all some day" (10), and Mrs. Compson nags at T. P. to be careful when they return home: "You'll turn us over" (12). Read metaphorically, this scene captures the declined aristocracy's certainty that blacks have an interest in dismantling tradition and stand ready to overturn their white superiors.

In complaining incessantly about their servants' unresponsiveness, the Compsons point to an apparent social upheaval. The vestigial gentility of the white, landholding aristocracy seems condemned to the twilight of its history. Mrs. Compson defends Jason's treatment of his niece and his domestic help when she reminds Dilsey that "He's head of the house now. It's his right to require us to respect his wishes. I try to do it, and if I can, you can too" (321). Jason's doom as head of this house could not be more certain. Mrs. Compson's having to remind subordinates of their duty to obey suggests how frail the dominant ideology has grown. Caddy's and her daughter's escapes weaken the patriarchy, just as Frony's relative independence signals a new age. Jason scorns his family's retention of an outmoded arrangement: "'You've got a prize set of servants,' Jason said. He helped his mother and himself to food. 'Did you ever have one that was worth killing? You must have had some before I was big enough to remember'" (322).

The signs of the old order's decay abound in *The Sound and the Fury*. Benjy and Luster play in the deserted barn beside the pasture the Compsons have sold. Mrs. Compson prides herself on her physical carriage, which distinguishes "our women" from "washerwomen" (72), and she refuses to use nicknames because "[o]nly common people use them" (73). When the New South was being constituted on the ruins of the old, the ideology of the surviving ruling class suffered extreme stress. The trauma of Reconstruction had made the possibility of a complete overturn of this ideology at least thinkable. Yet by the 1880s that ideology was in the process of aggressively refurbishing itself; mercantile and industrial capitalism stood ready to take over from antebellum slaveholding agrarian capitalism. To do so meant proposing that the new order would redeem and not repeat the failures of the defeated South. Thus the Compsons' nostalgia and outrage at the apparently final disappearance of the Old South in their way of life produces the conditions under which the Old South can become romanticized in the early decades of the twentieth century. The New South was a contradiction because it simultaneously forfeited and re-avowed the Old South. By adopting Yankee ways, the South hoped to reconstitute the prosperity and the dream that the North had destroyed.

The Sound and the Fury represents this process in the Blands of Kentucky, who caricature the gross idealization of aristocratic gentility. One hardly needs to elaborate on Quentin's ridicule of the South according to Gerald and his mother: "how Gerald throws his nigger downstairs and how the nigger plead to be allowed to matriculate in the divinity school to be near marster marse gerald and How he ran all the way to the station beside the carriage with tears in his eyes when marse gerald rid away" (122). Quentin sees in the Blands' laughable pretense—in their scorn for lower-class Yankees and their pride in caste and blood—how obsolete they are. What he cannot see, but Faulkner comprehends, is the way in which this vision of antebellum life continues to condition even those who think it no longer applies.

The Sound and the Fury suggests that nostalgia for an innocent manner of living—represented in the novel by Benjy's physical losses, Quentin's narcissistic hurt, and Jason's furious resentment—is a shield that hides the actual reimposition of a highly oppressive regime. The more the Compsons bemoan a lost purity and the more they abdicate to their overthrow by the formerly dispossessed, the more their class's ideology disguises its power to maintain the categories and mechanisms of the past. The Compson brothers all suffer from forms of dispossession that have social and economic consequences in addition to their more celebrated psychological ones. But even as Faulkner, whose own position in his society approximates theirs, notices these degradations, he also lets us see the resources for his class's and race's recovery.

The changes threatened in *The Sound and the Fury* involve the reversal of class hierarchy and the destabilization of racial categories. The novel constantly toys with the prospect that emancipation will make race a matter of behavior rather than genealogy. The Gibsons pride themselves on being "quality" because of their place in the Compson family. They repeatedly refer to lower-class blacks as "them niggers" (4); and Dilsey reproves Luster's disobedience by taking the tone of her masters' race: "Dont you sass me, nigger boy" (63). Correspondingly, whites who flout the code of social gentility are condemned as "niggers." Quentin at least mentally wonders to Caddy, "[w]hy must you do like nigger women do in the pasture"? (105); Jason warns his niece that "[w]hen people act like niggers, no matter who they are the only thing to do is treat them like a nigger" (208); and Uncle Maury's dependence on the Compsons provokes Mr. Compson's caustic appreciation of his brother-in-law, as if being a parasite is equivalent to being black: "He is invaluable to my own sense of racial superiority" (50).

These remarks reflect a world in which the mixture of races constitutes the future. How Quentin must recoil from Deacon's assurance that "you and me's the same folks, come long and short" (113), or from the Massachusetts boys' surprise that he "talks like a coloured man" (137). The white aristocracy's incensed dread produces Quentin's famous remark that "a nigger is not a person so much as a form of behaviour; a sort of obverse reflection of the white people he lives among" (98). Besides pointing to the familiar use of the racial Other as the psychological Other (see Irwin 1975), this statement also indicates the destabilizing of racial categories in the New South.

The most powerful agent for racial redefinition in the New South of *The Sound and the Fury* is economic reversal. Both the Compsons and their dependents register the social changes brought about by an apparent shift in economic modes. The white brothers notice throughout their section the tiny economic advances of their black retainers. Luster, in fact, begins the novel with a quest for financial recovery; he wants to find money that is rightfully his. The blacks' struggle for economic enfranchisement plays out across *The Sound and the Fury*. The black washwomen are doubtful of Luster's story and wonder if he has found the quarter "in white folks' pocket while they aint looking" (16). But Luster's response is disquietingly enigmatic; he has gotten that quarter, he says, "at the getting place," where there is "plenty more" (16). That blacks might have access to the getting place—in both the biological and financial senses, that is, access to both white women and white money—causes the master race to fear that the very sources of their authority are profoundly endangered. Back and forth the quarter jumps; it is retaken in the form of a stray golf ball by the white golfer, who simply annuls Luster's title to property (61). Luster muses that "[t]hat white man hard to get along with" (62), a reminder that racial relations are inseparable from economic ones. Finally, after Jason destroys his free passes because Luster cannot pay for them, Dilsey manages to get another quarter from Frony, and Luster goes to the show.

This fable of economic independence and access to leisure suggests the transformation whites feared, the day when "[n]igger's money good as white folks" (17). The Compsons think they are becoming poor, and so "black," just as blacks are becoming economically independent, and so "white." Under Luster's hand, Benjy plays the role of the dispossessed master: the heir-never-to-be still thinks, idiotically, that *they own this pasture* (22). "Mulehead," as Luster once calls his charge (57), paces the Compson grounds like a master-turned-slave; he is never let off the place; he is sent out into the cold; and, when he starts to complain about his suffering, Luster threatens to whip him. Like Jim Bond, the mentally retarded mulatto great grandson of plantation master Thomas Sutpen in *Absalom, Absalom!*, Benjy becomes the enfeebled dependent of those his line has sought to subjugate. It is no wonder that the Compsons' dread of such a reversal produces a picture of Luster enjoying the leisure formerly reserved for white masters. In *Absalom* the young Sutpen aspires to the wealthy planter Pettibone's hammock as the symbol of mastery and prosperity, but in *The Sound and the Fury* "[t]here was a hammock made of barrel staves slatted into woven wires. Luster lay down in the swing, but Ben went on vaguely and purposely. He began to whimper again. 'Hush, now,' Luster said, 'I fixin to whup you'" (364).

This apparently new confusion of race and economic status in the South may also be seen in Quentin's attitude toward Deacon. When Shreve jokes about "what your grandpa did to that poor old nigger," Quentin retorts, "Now he can spend day after day marching in parades. If it hadn't been for my grandfather, he'd have to work like whitefolks" (94). Quentin goes on to complain about how even "working nigger[s]" can never be found when you want them, "let alone one that lived off the fat of the land" (94). Quentin's racial hostility derives from economic anxiety. Deacon's parasitism goads Quentin; Deacon's "chicanery" lets him "young marster" the southern sons of Harvard until he had "completely subjugated" them and "had bled" them until they learned better (111).

The North presents Quentin with the spectacle of racial and economic reversal: when he gets on a streetcar full of "mostly prosperous looking people," he takes the only vacant seat—"beside a nigger" (97). After a while, Quentin notices that he is riding into lower-class areas; "men in work-clothes were beginning to outnumber the shined shoes and collars" (101). At this moment, "[t]he nigger touched my knee. 'Pardon me,' he said. I swung my legs out and let him pass" (101). That the black might pass—pass as white, work to pass by his former masters—informs Quentin's phobias. This conflation of economic and racial amalgamation applies to his treatment of the little Italian girl as well.

Quentin responds ambivalently to the immigrant's appearance. Although he sympathizes with her poverty, he also recoils from the touch of her hot, damp, dirty fingers; when she opens her palm to pay, Quentin can smell her coin, "faintly metallic" (145). Others, like the storekeeper, complain more directly about "them foreigners," but Quentin, too, seems disturbed by the economic aspirations of the newly enfranchised—"Land of the kike home of the wop," he muses as he regards the child's face (144). The girl's foreignness to Quentin picks up an odd racial cast in his descriptions of her. He says that her "face was like a cup of milk dashed with coffee" (143). This epithet is used for only one other character in *The Sound and the Fury*, the pastor of the black church, who is "of a light coffee colour" (338). Quentin repeatedly describes the immigrant girl's "black" looks (147, 149, 152, 157, 158), and I think this adjective points to the way all foreign elements that threaten his world order are in effect black. Seeing that the future will continue to desecrate his ideal of the South, Quentin commits suicide on 2 June, the eve of Jefferson Davis's birthday.

Jason extends this racial image of economic reversal as he seethes about the last of the Compsons having "to work all day long in a damn store" (238). His cracks about putting Benjy on the night shift or renting him to a sideshow underscore his outrage that the Compsons have fallen into the laboring class. Jason conceives of his misfortune in the South's only operative categories of labor: slavery and mastery. Caroline can see that her son must "slave" his life away for the family's survival (208, 285). But Jason's outlook is contradictory because he denies his status as a slave to wage earning even as he aspires to win back all that lost luxury and leisure. Jason sneers that unlike his father he does not have an office (208), yet he refuses to acknowledge that his privileged days have all but ended. Like a hard-pressed plantation owner, Jason complains about a kitchen full of "niggers to feed" (214) and simply refuses to do work that is beneath him, such as mounting a spare tire. He puts Earl on notice that unlike his employer, Jason Compson will "never be a slave to any business" (242). Jason acts the part of the declined aristocrat, hoping to evade the paradox that to recover what he has lost, he must work like the dispossessed while behaving like the ruling class.

Such a contradiction accounts for Jason's railing at both the enjoyment of leisure and the exertions of labor. Jason indicts poor blacks for their laziness and dependence: "let these damn trifling niggers starve for a couple of years, then they'd see what a soft thing they have" (219). He cannot understand why they abandon farm work to see a show. Yet he also complains about the "damn foreigner" Jews and insiders who trick hardworking honest investors like Jason out of their money, forcing them into bondage to the market. As the survivor of a ruling class, Jason recognizes only his own entitlement (as capitalist rather than worker) to leisure and to the fruits of others' labor.

The contradictions of the Compson brothers' minds display the contradictions of their class's ideology. Their shared sense that a world has been lost, that they are in the throes of a social upheaval, conceals the mechanisms by which the dominant ideology retools itself for the new age. That the Compsons understand their dispossession as a reversal means that they do not entertain any change in the categories of economic production and social arrangement. Blacks may become white, the poor wealthy, but life will still be organized by competition, racial differentiation, the enjoyment of leisure at the expense of others.

Surely the Compson Appendix confirms this trajectory. We learn that Jason Compson IV as of 1945 has worked his way from hardware clerk to owner of a farmers' supply store and dealer in cotton. C. Vann Woodward and economic historians of the New South have observed the ways in which the lien system was the economic bane of agriculture in the New South. In many regions this system elevated a new group to privilege; they took over the means of agricultural production by extending credit or percentage arrangements to farmers. Sometimes former plantation owners grabbed this new method of control over what the land produced, though more commonly newcomers like the Varners or Snopeses emerged. (Faulkner chronicles the rise of one such poor white clan, the Snopeses, in a trilogy of novels: *The Hamlet* [1940], *The Town* [1957], and *The Mansion* [1959].) We are told in the Compson Appendix that Jason competes successfully for a while with "internal immigrants" like the Snopeses. He does so by preying on the economically dependent, who turn out to be none other than "Negro Mississippi farmers" (Appendix, NCE, 230). Though the male

Compson line will end with the heirless Jason, *The Sound and the Fury* sees that the racial and economic structure of the New South resembles awfully its origins in what *Absalom, Absalom!* calls the "theater for violence and injustice and bloodshed," where "the sheen on the dollars was not from gold but from blood" (*Absalom*, 250).

The Compson Appendix and *Absalom* suggest a second way in which *The Sound and the Fury* proper represses contradictions, making the reality of history apparent between the lines. For if the dominant ideology conceals its governance of the New South by pretending its day has passed, so also does that ideology's defense of antebellum life deny the economic and racial realities of agrarian slaveholding capitalism. The fundamental contradictions of this world become the subject of Faulkner's conscious meditations on southern history in *Absalom*, which have been most ably elucidated in Carolyn Porter's (1981) analysis of that novel. But in *The Sound and the Fury* the lessons of cultural injustice fall on deaf ears. At a few points in Quentin's section, for example, the prose crinkles on the verge of making a connection between the private obsession with Caddy's purity and the larger questions of the South. Once, Quentin remembers his father's remark that *"You will find that even injustice is scarcely worthy of what you believe yourself to be"* (141). A little later, Quentin notices that the baker lady looks like a librarian, custodian of "dusty shelves of ordered certitudes long divorced from reality, desiccating peacefully, as if a breath of that air which sees injustice done" (143). The novel is inhospitable to the history of injustice because that history everywhere seeks to invade the novel. The air that sees injustice done seems to Quentin to be entombed in books decaying safely unread on their shelves.

Like the whole novel, Quentin's mind tries to remain oblivious to history. The student remembers daydreaming in class, until he is recalled by the teacher's sarcastic reproof: "Tell Quentin who discovered the Mississippi River, Henry" (100). One has only seven years to wait for another Henry, this one a Sutpen, to get Quentin to listen to things Mississippian. But in *The Sound and the Fury* history makes itself felt by being forgotten, by making itself into a background blur.

6

appreciating the technique

By this stage in our discussion of *The Sound and the Fury* it may seem artificial or even redundant to devote a separate section to Faulkner's technique. I have tried to emphasize throughout that the novel's meaning remains inseparable from the style and form in which it is presented. Few would argue with such a view of any literary work, of course; nonetheless, modernist artworks like *The Sound and the Fury* make the processes of literary production more apparent than works we consider realistic. At the same time, literary realism in the nineteenth and twentieth centuries relies no less on conventions of representation. Since all literature is made of language, with its encoding of experiences and objects, every work must be approached partly through the codes of representation it uses. The literature of periods other than the modernist, moreover, may call our attention to the processes of representation as well; in the English novel one might think of two eighteenth-century works: the epistolary novel *Clarissa* by Samuel Richardson or *Tristram Shandy* by Laurence Sterne, whose self-reflective technique more closely resembles that of our contemporary John Barth than any work that fell between the two.

Readers have rather uniformly sensed that the technique of *The*

Sound and the Fury bears a specially urgent relation to the subject matter of the novel. Though Faulkner's account of trying to write the same story four times and failing each time may not be literally accurate, it does suggest the fragmentary, open form of the novel he produced. As for any author, Faulkner's books came to him in different ways. Some, like *The Sound and the Fury*, he felt take shape under his hand as he wrote them. One of Faulkner's more comical analogies for the writer's enterprise is that it is like building a henhouse in a hurricane; the writer reaches for this plank and that while holding a piece or two in place as he hammers. Such a description points to the surprises that lie ahead of the author as he sees where his book is headed. A few years after writing *The Sound and the Fury*, Faulkner remembered experiencing similar sensations while writing *Light in August:* "I waited almost two years, then I began Light in August, knowing no more about it than a young woman, pregnant, walking along a strange country road. . . . [I thought,] I know no more about this book than I did about The Sound and The Fury when I sat down before the first blank page" ("An Introduction," *Southern Review,* 709; NCE, 219). On the other hand, Faulkner experienced some of his acts of composition as much more premeditated: thinking back on *As I Lay Dying*, Faulkner says that "[b]efore I ever put pen to paper and set down the first word, I knew what the last word would be and almost where the last period would fall" ("An Introduction," *Southern Review,* 709; NCE, 219). And the walls of Faulkner's study at Rowanoak, his house in Oxford, today bear witness to the deliberate planning of his much later novel *A Fable;* on them are preserved Faulkner's handwritten outline for the events of the novel day by day.

STYLE

Whatever legend Faulkner spins around the improvisatory nature of its composition, *The Sound and the Fury* in its final form displays careful patterns of organization. Looking back across the novel, we can appreciate the astonishing variety of its four styles. Every reader recognizes the simplicity of Benjy's manner of speech, but a study by L. Moffitt Cecil (1970) provides statistical confirmation: he finds that Benjy's working vocabulary amounts to only five hundred words, most of them verbs and nouns. The infant-man's incapacity to render his world with much nuance is reflected by Benjy's confinement to only about one hundred modifiers (adjectives and adverbs). Similarly, the first section plays and replays Benjy's favorite images (Cecil traces the phrase "bright shapes" as an example), suggesting a mind governed, as we have seen, by a few fundamental longings and sensations. Benjy's grammatical patterns are as simple as his vocabulary; though not all of his sentences are subject-verb-object kernels, he can manage only about seventy complex ones (those with subordinate clauses).

Quentin's section impresses us as the most stylistically ambitious. Besides the associative range of his memory—drawing together the most disparate events and words so long as they are touched by Caddy's aura—Quentin's section showcases Faulkner's most advanced experiment with stream-of-consciousness writing; we have seen how Quentin's thoughts run by submerging past and present moments into the undifferentiated flux of his mind. Though much of the section's language never leaves Quentin's mind, most readers assume that it reflects Quentin's powers of expression. Faulkner even considered Quentin the shadow narrator of the novel: "Then it needs the protagonist, someone to tell the story, so Quentin appeared" (Bleikasten 1982, 16).

We have already seen how Quentin's habits of observation and comprehension imitate an author's. For example, he selects images that organize his sensations—timepieces, the gull, the clock's chimes, shadows. These images structure and embody the preoccupations of his mind in a process inseparable from the production of his section; that is, Quentin's mind, like the minds of his brothers, is indistinguishable from the words on the page on which it is inscribed. The "mind" of the novel becomes coextensive with the minds of the characters. In Quentin's case, we see a remarkably observant, connective mentality, one whose powers resemble an author's, but whose will to recount the past—and, in doing so, to reconstruct, to change, in effect to lose it—differs importantly from his creator's (see Pitavy 1982 on Quentin the failed lyric poet).

As we have seen, Quentin's plight derives from his conviction that none of the "certitudes" (143) of his world any longer holds true:

> I would lie in bed thinking when will it stop when will it stop. The draft in the door smelled of water, a damp steady breath. Sometimes I could put myself to sleep saying that over and over until after the honeysuckle got all mixed up in it the whole thing came to symbolise night and unrest I seemed to be lying neither asleep nor awake looking down a long corridor of grey halflight where all stable things had become shadowy paradoxical all I had done shadows all I had felt suffered taking visible form antic and perverse mocking without relevance inherent themselves with the denial of the significance they should have affirmed thinking I was I was not who was not was not who. (194)

I quoted part of this passage earlier to illustrate Quentin's confusion over a world that seems suddenly inverted by his sister's defiance of their common code of honor and morality, a confusion that runs down to the very foundation of Quentin's sense of identity ("I was I was not who was not was not who"). The style of the passage typifies the workings of Quentin's mind in other ways as well. Lying in bed, Quentin wonders when the smell of rain-sodden wistaria will stop invading his room; but the "it" acquires other meanings. "It" is the smell of water, too, and a moment later Quentin is thinking, "I could smell the curves of the river beyond the dusk" (195). The Charles River, in which he will commit suicide, carries the same scent of death that arises from the waters of the rain and the branch, which soak and muddy Caddy. Indeed, "it" might easily refer to the inexorable processes of maturation, sexuality, pregnancy, time, and history that Quentin finds responsible for altering his world beyond recognition.

This use of "it" is a good example of what we might call Quentin's overdetermined style, each word or thought radiating his essential preoccupations. Some of these preoccupations float on the surface of his language; we know that Caddy's loss haunts him and forces onto him questions of mortality, physical passion, and identity. Some of his preoccupations, on the other hand, remain invisible to him; we have seen in chapter 4 that the characters, especially Quentin, take their predicament as universal and so never realize that their story represents the fate of a particular social arrangement at a particular moment in history. Quentin believes his infatuation with his sister's virginity "symbolise[s]" the "denial" of all "significance" (like Shakespeare's "full of sound and fury, / Signifying nothing"), but the reader is in a position to judge a specific class, race, and gender's narrow self-interested defense of the ways that benefit them.

In the above passage, then, we might note a vocabulary of mystification, words that emphasize the unintelligibility of what is happening to Quentin: "all mixed up," "the whole thing," "I seemed," "neither asleep nor awake," "grey halflight," "shadowy paradoxical," "mocking without relevance," and so on. Likewise, the verb tenses of these lines accord with Quentin's bafflement; they alternate between an incurably nostalgic past tense ("Sometimes I could put myself to sleep") and a present tense consisting of participals ("saying," "taking," and so on) that keep Quentin locked in a murky ongoing present, as if he is submerged in a process whose beginning and end he cannot fathom. In diction and syntax of this sort Quentin habitually translates his misery into terms that obscure it from analysis. We might wonder if such a tendency does not help to separate the poetic but immaturely despairing Quentin Compson from the young William Faulkner who both resembles him and must leave him behind as he matures in his own powers of artistry.

Quentin's eventual suicide may be forecast from the shrinking of his ego throughout his section. Not only does Quentin frequently consider the instability of his "I" (as in the last lines quoted above), he also seems less and less an agent of action than one acted upon. We can see this stylistically in the stream-of-consciousness passages toward the end of Quentin's section. Quentin slips into a remembered conversation with his father: "Just by imagining the clump it seemed to me that I could hear whispers secret surges smell the beating of hot blood under wild unsecret flesh watching against red eyelids the swine untethered in pairs rushing coupled into the sea and he we must just stay awake and see evil done for a little while its not always and i it doesn't have to be even that long for a man of courage" (202). Notice how the imagery of sexual passion ("surges," "beating of hot blood") merges with that of degradation and death ("swine untethered in pairs rushing coupled into the sea"). (Here Quentin refers to a Greek legend in which the swineherd Eubuleus chances to be tending his herd at the moment when Pluto, king of the underworld, carries off Persephone in a fit of lust. A chasm opens to allow the couple's passage into the underworld, and Eubuleus' herd is swallowed up.) The "i" of the passage belongs to Quentin, but significantly it has become lowercase, as if indicating its imminent disappearance. Father's voice has become so much a part of Quentin's mentality that he (and we) can hardly separate the two strands of speech. The conversation has been so internalized that it suggests how completely the voices of Quentin's world have overpowered him. Quentin's style dramatizes the engulfment of his ego in statements and behavior dictated by others (see Ross 1975).

If Benjy's style impressionistically records his world, and Quentin's more expressionistically transforms it into private reverie, Jason's style pretends to some kind of communication. He is the first narrator to have an awareness of audience. Jason's section sounds like someone telling the story of his life in such a way as to explain his sorry lot and justify his behavior. From his first words, Jason presents himself as the speaker of what we are reading: "Once a bitch always a bitch, *what I say. I says* you're lucky if her playing out of school is all that worries you. *I says*" (206, emphasis added). As part of his campaign to assure us that he is the only sane, responsible Compson left, Jason takes us into his confidence, quoting himself continuously as the inside authority on his family, town, and South.

Because he is much more aware that his statements are being heard by others, Jason relies on a vocabulary common to his

community. His language teems with colloquial expressions ("Her kimono came unfastened, flapping about her, *damn near* naked") and
automatically resorts to the social designations a small-town southern
white male might have used in 1928: "redneck," "nigger," "Jew,"
"bitch," and so on. Jason pours out a torrent of bigotry, envy, and
resentment; the breathlessness of his speech suggests the barely re-
strained madness just below his bourgeois correctness. Notice how in
the following passage Jason begins to lose control of his language as
he fumes over his niece's public misbehavior.

> I went on to the street, but they were out of sight. And there I was,
> without any hat, looking like I was crazy too. Like a man would
> naturally think, one of them is crazy and another one drowned him-
> self and the other one was turned out into the street by her husband,
> what's the reason the rest of them are not crazy too. All the time I
> could see them watching me like a hawk, waiting for a chance to
> say Well I'm not surprised I expected it all the time the whole fam-
> ily's crazy. Selling land to send him to Harvard and paying taxes to
> support a state University all the time that I never saw except twice
> at a baseball game and not letting her daughter's name be spoken
> on the place until after a while Father wouldn't even come down
> town anymore but just sat there all day with the decanter I could
> see the bottom of his nightshirt and his bare legs and hear the de-
> canter clinking until finally T. P. had to pour it for him and she says
> You have no respect for your Father's memory and I says I dont
> know why not it sure is preserved well enough to last only if I'm
> crazy too God knows what I'll do about it just to look at water
> makes me sick. (268–69)

Jason here falls into his own version of stream of consciousness. Such
moments do not appear often in his section, but when they do, they
follow the same logic we have noticed in his brothers' sections. Like
Quentin, Jason appears abnormally influenced by what others will say
and do about his behavior. Unlike Quentin, however, Jason wants to
live his life in accordance with the public morals and customs of his
community. He tries to uphold the decent life as dictated by the petit
bourgeois mentality that prevails in Jefferson; the periodic disruptions

of his ungovernable family get reflected in the periodic disruptions of his syntax. His patient explanation to any who will listen tries to hold to orderly, grammatical sentences. But the chaos engulfing him draws out an excessive, nonstop protest over his victimization. His niece's behavior opens the gates in his mind, and soon he is running back over his whole history of slights and dispossession. Here the past and the present merge in a way quite reminiscent of Quentin's mind. We can appreciate how much effort it costs Jason to remain the only apparently sane Compson (as Faulkner called him some years later in the Compson Appendix).

Jason's storytelling does not succeed finally as a form of communication. The fate of the stories he tells to other characters reinforces his sense of futility; as he explains, for example, why the sheriff should accompany him in pursuing the runaway Quentin, he realizes that he will have to start over for the resistant hearer: "He repeated the story, harshly recapitulant, seeming to get an actual pleasure out of his outrage and impotence" (351). Jason's story has no practical effect; the sheriff refuses his request. We may suspect that Jason's entire narrative section, like this performance, is designed less to inform and convince another than to hoard and pore over his misery. Another private celebration of loss, Jason's section finally seems less heard than overheard.

The regularity of the style of the last section, as we have remarked earlier, strikes the reader. Its diction belongs to the tradition of literary language; it possesses a somber dignity that sounds authoritative: "The day dawned bleak and chill . . ." The opening sentence unfurls around the figure of Dilsey, not only describing her outwardly, as we have seen, but doing so in a highly considered language. Like Faulkner's prose in other novels, the style depends on Latinate vocabulary: "dissolving" "disintegrate," "venomous," "particles," and so on. The style aims at visual precision ("one gaunt hand flac-soled as the belly of a fish" [306]) and becomes populous with similes and descriptive analogies.

Yet even "Faulkner"'s voice does not enjoy ultimate authority to render the world of *The Sound and the Fury*. We have seen how the language that describes the Easter sermon, for example, signals its unfamiliarity with the experiences and point of view of the black congregants. Even though much of the section's action adopts Dilsey's perspective (following her through her morning, seeming to convey a sense of her thoughts), not all of the narrative is centered in Dilsey's consciousness. Since Dilsey does not narrate the section (as the Compson brothers do theirs), we must admit that she cannot claim equivalent authority over a version of the events. The narrative of the last section focalizes in her (we see things filtered through her), but even that situation grows complicated when the narrative abandons her for a while to follow Jason's pursuit of Quentin. During these pages, the narrative focalizes in Jason again. Such a distribution of the narrative suggests that no telling is final or uniform.

One stylistic marker of this situation appears in the drawing on p. 360. Jason sees "a sign in electric lights" in which the device "of a human eye with an electric pupil" substitutes for the word "eye" in an advertisement. The novel reproduces the pictorial eye, suggesting that words fail meaning at this point, that the novel must resort to a kind of rebus language (in which things represent themselves). In addition, we may notice that the novel refers to the drawn eye as a "gap," which implies a blank space. Only from the standpoint of written language, of course, can the eye be considered a gap. It is as if Faulkner emphasizes here the segregation of two modes of representation, a gesture that reminds us of what another Faulkner character says: "words dont ever fit even what they are trying to say at" (*As I Lay Dying*, 157). Perhaps this is the fitting last word on the styles of *The Sound and the Fury*.

STRUCTURE

Whatever thematic repetition, narrative technique, or verbal patterns we may detect from section to section of *The Sound and the Fury*, no one can deny that fragmentation remains its dominant effect. In perhaps the best study of this issue, Donald M. Kartiganer argues that the novel is Faulkner's diagnosis of modern alienation and isolation: "*The Sound and the Fury* is Faulkner's version of a waste-land fiction, an irredeemably broken sequence of speakers and narrative episodes. Each of the four secitons seems locked within itself—interpenetration at an absolute minimum—and none of the narrators, even the 'author' in the fourth section, is able to escape the confines of his private vision" (1970, 619). The novel fails to cohere around any single principle or set of organizing principles—at least among the terms suggested by the novel itself. Even Caddy, who serves as the focal interest for the three Compson brothers, does not really fix the attention of the last section. Faulkner's reading of the novel as "manufacturing" his heart's darling—the sister he never had and the daughter he was to lose in infancy—and as telling the story of her disappearance four times, even this interpretation distorts what we actually find in *The Sound and the Fury.*

The status of the scene that Faulkner claimed generated the novel might typify the fragmentary nature of the novel. The sight of Caddy's muddy drawers suspended above the gazing brothers as she looks in on Damuddy's funeral constitutes the novel's master scene according to Faulkner. But that scene appears fully only in the first section, only implicitly in Quentin's section, and inversely in the last section, when Caddy's daughter climbs down the same tree to make her escape from her Uncle Jason. So, as Kartiganer concludes, "rather than a means of binding the fragments together, the image is itself complicated by the fragmentation; finally it moves into that isolation within the memory, eternal and not quite relevant, which all the major images of the novel possess" (1970, 619–20).

The image of Caddy in the tree struggles to find a symbolic context in which it might make larger sense. On the margins of the scene appear reminders of another scene in which a disobedient female fatally touches a tree of knowledge. The episode begins as "a snake crawled out from under the house" (42). Caddy says she is not afraid of snakes though Jason is. When Caddy begins climbing, Versh reminds her that "Your paw told you to stay out that tree." "That was a long time ago," she responds. "I expect he's forgotten about it" (44). Discovering Caddy in the tree, Dilsey shouts at her, "You, Satan. . . . Come down from there" (51). Caddy returns to her male cohorts with knowledge of the mystery of death, a knowledge, as we have seen, inseparable from that of sex. It is no wonder that Caddy soon offers to initiate the adolescent Quentin into the experience she has passed through, and no wonder that her brother thinks of her as "the voice o'er Eden."

Putting these references together, we may see that Faulkner wants to recall the scene of Eve's temptation by Satan in the Garden of Eden. *Genesis*'s account of the human fall into sin would explain Caddy's affinity for evil as a consequence and a reenactment of that original sin. The death and resurrection of Jesus is interpreted by the writers of the New Testament as a redemption of the fall, and that event serves as both the backdrop for the setting of the novel across Easter weekend 1928 and the subject of Rev. Shegog's sermon. Yet the fall and redemption story's particles do not cohere within the novel, and the reader may be left to conclude that such a universal explanation of the Compsons' predicament cannot address the particular features that spell their doom: the shifts in economic, social, racial, and gender realities that appear only to them and their kind as "all time and injustice and sorrow" (333).

Maurice Coindreau (1966), Faulkner's French translator, ingeniously likens the four-part structure of the novel to a symphony. Each section he considers a movement with its own tempo and form: the first movement is a *moderato* that introduces the major themes of the rest of the work; the second, "the painful *Adagio*, explores Quentin's black despair"; Jason's "movement" drives a frenzied *Allegro;* and the last section breaks into three subdivisions—Quentin's escape in *Allegro furioso*, Shegog's sermon as an *Andante religioso*, and an *Allegro barbaro* ending in "the calm of a *Lento*" (see Coindreau 1966). Though Faulkner always professed to be less interested in music than the visual arts, Coindreau's analogy is not wholly fanciful and does suggest the abstract quality of Faulkner's fiction. Walter Pater, a late nineteenth-century writer on the arts, suggested that all literature aspired to the condition of music.

Appreciating the Technique

Such scaffolds for the novel, however much readers may decide they pertain to its meaning, serve largely to measure the centrifugal impulses of *The Sound and the Fury*. None of the schemes of organization readers have proposed fully replaces the apparent unity of impression created by the traditional realistic narrative; nor, as we have seen, is such unity Faulkner's goal.

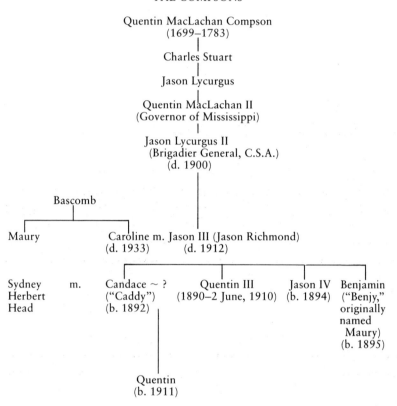

THE COMPSONS

Quentin MacLachan Compson
(1699–1783)

Charles Stuart

Jason Lycurgus

Quentin MacLachan II
(Governor of Mississippi)

Jason Lycurgus II
(Brigadier General, C.S.A.)
(d. 1900)

Bascomb

Maury

Caroline m. Jason III (Jason Richmond)
(d. 1933)   (d. 1912)

Sydney   m.   Candace ~ ?   Quentin III   Jason IV   Benjamin
Herbert   ("Caddy")   (1890–2 June, 1910)   (b. 1894)   ("Benjy,"
Head   (b. 1892)   originally
                                                                named
                                                                Maury)
                                                                (b. 1895)

Quentin
(b. 1911)

(~ = sexual relation with unmarried partner)

THE GIBSONS

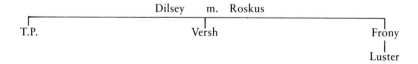

Dilsey   m.   Roskus

T.P.   Versh   Frony

Luster

Material drawn from Brooks 1973, 447, who infers dates from *The Sound and the Fury*, "That Evening Sun" (*Collected Stories*), and the Compson Appendix.

7

faulkner's further reflections

In summarizing his efforts to get *The Sound and the Fury* "right" by telling it four different ways, Faulkner wonders whether any novel is ever "finished," or is it it rather just "abandoned?" Faulkner means to call attention to the disparity between the artistic rendition of experience and the unceasing flow of experience itself. In one of his most famous remarks about his objectives as a writer, Faulkner remarked that the "aim of every artist is to arrest motion" (*Lion*, 253). Almost by definition, then, the work of art cannot help distorting reality even as it represents it. At the same time, such "distortion" is precisely what makes reality comprehensible and intelligible to the reader, who must detach himself or herself from experience to reflect upon it: Quentin Compson muses in *Absalom, Absalom!* about the events he is narrating, "If I had been there I could not have seen it this plain" (*Absalom*, 238).

One of the distinctive features of Faulkner's fiction is that characters and settings make repeated appearances throughout his career. Many of his novels and short stories concentrate on a few fictional families—the Sartorises, Compsons, Sutpens, Snopeses, McCaslins—in the town of Jefferson and its environs. Faulkner called this whole interrelated world Yoknapatawpha County, signing his name as "sole owner and proprietor" on the map of the county he drew as an end-piece for the first edition of *Absalom, Absalom!* Because Faulkner considered Yoknapatawpha a region with its own continuing history, his novels revisit it freely to tell new portions of its story. Moreover, whatever discrepancies arise from work to work over the more than three decades of Yoknapatawpha fiction Faulkner attributed to his knowing the characters better than he did before.

Faulkner reconsidered the Compson material in at least three important ways after *The Sound and the Fury* was published in 1929. One further reflection involves his use of Quentin Compson as a narrator in several short stories that appeared in the 1930s. The first of these, "That Evening Sun," was published in 1930 in H. L. Mencken's *American Mercury*. (The periodical version of the story was actually entitled "That Evening Sun Go Down"; it also bears some revisions suggested by Mencken to tone down the sexual explicitness of the story. Faulkner eliminated these changes in the version eventually published in the 1950 *Collected Stories*.) In "That Evening Sun," an older Quentin (age twenty-four) tells the story of the Compsons' black laundrywoman, Nancy, whose estranged husband, Jesus, threatens to murder her. Nancy is carrying the child of a white townsman who has paid her for sexual relations. The story is a remarkable study in dread as it concentrates on Nancy's predicament, but it also portrays a kind of postsuicide Quentin who mourns the simpler way of southern small-town life that is being replaced by automobiles, telephones, and—implicitly—a whole social order in which racial and gender relations are now troubled (at least for those enjoying positions of superiority).

Quentin also narrates two other short stories, "A Justice" (appearing in the collection *These Thirteen* in 1931) and "Lion" (appearing in 1935 in *Harper's*). In both, Quentin narrates episodes of his community's history. "A Justice" involves the settlement of a dispute between a black slave of an Indian king and a half-breed Indian over a black slave woman. The story is richly ambiguous, for it invites two contradictory interpretations. One interpretation is that the Indian king, whose nickname is Doom, protects the rights of even a black slave to defend his wife from the Indian Craw-ford's advances. There is also evidence, however, that Doom sets up Craw-ford as the suspected father of the "yellow" child the slave bears to hide his own use of the woman behind her husband's back. (In the story proper there is only the hint of Doom's self-interest in deciding the case as he does. But in a later story, "The Old People," included in *Go Down, Moses*, Faulkner reveals that Doom, and not Craw-ford, is actually the father of the child.) Quentin's telling of this story, then, exposes part of the long legacy of racial and sexual exploitation, but with the difference that here red men, not white men, are at fault. The story tends to universalize, and so perhaps soften, the crimes of oppression that Quentin is coming to confront in the history of his own race.

"Lion" also enables Quentin to hide from history, in this case as he returns to the timeless wilderness as a member of an annual hunting party. The mythical standing of the big woods and the eternal rounds of pursuit of Old Ben, the elusive king bear of the forest, seem to constitute a sanctuary from the modern world of economic and racial strife. In the woods, there seems to be one anonymous brotherhood. Yet the story shows the persistent traces of racial hierarchy, servitude, and willful obliviousness to social reality.

Sketchy as my treatment of these stories must be, it can demonstrate Faulkner's continued interest in presenting Quentin as a witness to the injustices of the tradition that has formed him. Yet Quentin remains resistant to fully confronting that history; instead, he enshrouds himself in nostalgia, denial, and ambiguity, almost, we might say, deadening himself to the consequences of his region's past. Faulkner makes that deadening effect literal in these short stories by having Quentin survive, as it were, his own suicide in *The Sound and the Fury*.

More spectacularly yet, Faulkner resurrects Quentin and his father to serve as principal narrators in *Absalom, Absalom!* (1936). The events of that novel are divided between Sutpen's life (1809–69) and two days of telling about those events in the fall of 1909 and January of 1910. So the Quentin who helps tell Sutpen's story has not yet reached 2 June 1910, the date of his section in *The Sound and the Fury* and the eve of his suicide. Quentin's attitude in his sections of *Absalom* resembles his narrative stances in the short stories. Many of the Compsons' own problems reappear in the stories Mr. Compson and Quentin create and listen to. Sutpen's story begins with his arrival in Jefferson as a penniless twenty-five-year-old in 1833. Gradually he tames a one hundred-square-mile plot of land, raises a mansion, establishes a cotton plantation, and amasses a fortune. To this incarnation of southern splendor he seeks to add a wife, Ellen Coldfield, and progeny, especially sons.

Mysteriously, however, the planned marriage of Sutpen's daughter Judith to a New Orleanian named Charles Bon is forbidden by the father, delayed by the Civil War (during which Bon and his would-be brother-in-law Henry fight side by side), and resolved by Henry's apparently inexplicable murder of Charles at the gate to Sutpen's Hundred when they return from the war. Rosa Coldfield, Sutpen's sister-in-law, tells the first version of the story to Quentin. She has been a casualty of Sutpen's arrogance, having heard the desperate widower propose a trial mating with her to see if they might produce a male heir to Sutpen's domain. (By murdering Bon Henry has renounced his birthright and become a fugitive from the law.) Quentin listens to a story of disappointed love, virginal isolation, and the folly of defending a sister's honor—all material he deals with in *The Sound and the Fury*.

Mr. Compson's portion of the narrative deepens our appreciation of the ways in which *Absalom* helps to put the Compson family into an historical framework. He concentrates on questions of incest, suicide, and despair, hoping in part to give the son listening to him strategies for coping with the disillusionment of having been born a ghost into a world obsessed with past defeat and doubtful of the future. Mr. Compson tries to convince Quentin that human exertion "doesn't matter," that the story of the South is hardly coherent let alone cause for self-condemnation. But Quentin sees—especially as he helps his Harvard roommate, Shreve, tell the story—that the South has been founded on legacies of social injustice and immense personal suffering.

As in the other works he narrates, Quentin is finally put into the position of having to deny his deep resentment of what the South has made him. The novel closes with Quentin's scarcely believable protest: "*I dont hate the South. I dont hate it*" (*Absalom*, 471).

The last significant reconsideration of the Compsons in Faulkner's career appeared in an anthology of his work in 1946. Malcolm Cowley, a critic and editor who had long admired Faulkner's fiction, was dismayed to discover that all of Faulkner's novels—with the exception of *Sanctuary*—were out of print by the end of World War II. Cowley launched plans for Viking Press to issue a volume of excerpts from Faulkner's work in their Viking Portable series. In editing the book, Cowley opened a correspondence with Faulkner. In the course of their exchanges over information Cowley needed to write his introduction, he asked Faulkner if he might not like to write a brief headnote for the portions to be drawn from *The Sound and the Fury*. Cowley thought this key to the characters would enable first-time readers to grasp Faulkner's difficult novel more readily.

Faulkner agreed to write the piece, and the result was an "Appendix" (the Compson Appendix) to *The Sound and the Fury* that was much longer than planned. In some subsequent reissues of the novel, though not in the *Viking Portable Faulkner*, this appendix appeared as a headnote, a preface or introductory segment. Such an arrangement, while certainly easing the reader's passage into Faulkner's great experimentalist text, nonetheless short-circuited the intended shock and confusion Benjy's section was as surely meant to produce. Subsequent editions like the widely available Vintage paperback included the appendix as an afterword to the novel's four sections. More recently, Noel Polk has decided in the course of entirely reediting the novel that the appendix should not appear as a part of *The Sound and the Fury*. Faulkner's addition of what is in effect another part of his novel after sixteen years presents us with a critical dilemma that cannot be settled with a single solution. Any author's revision of a work— no matter how much later it follows the original version—must be treated seriously. Yet such an alteration through revision or addition ought not to tempt us to ignore the work as it was known originally.

Perhaps in some cases we must consider "the work" not merely as what appears between two covers at a moment in time but as a set of formal responses to a given body of material. Any of Faulkner's novels may be dealt with separately, but some of them may also be dealt with as parts of a larger whole. (This is manifestly true for the novels of the Snopes trilogy—*The Hamlet, The Town,* and *The Mansion*—which deal with the rise of Flem Snopes and his poor white family.)

The appendix to *The Sound and the Fury* emphasizes certain elements of the Compson story that are only implied in the novel proper. After writing *Absalom, Absalom!*, Faulkner was in a position to see that the Compsons' brand of aristocratic honor and morality actually rested upon—and perhaps even helped to conceal—a legacy of financial, racial, and political opportunism. Most of the Compson Appendix is devoted to recording the generations of the New World Compsons, who arrive in the person of Quentin MacLachan Compson, "a Glasgow printer" who in the eighteenth century flees from Scotland to Carolina to escape the consequences of fighting against English domination. (Southerners who could point to Scottish heritage, like the Falkners, were very proud of this connection; the lost cause of Confederate opposition to Yankee "invasion" was often justified by likening it to Scottish combat with the English (see Dekker 1987). The Glasgow Quentin's grandson, Jason Lycurgus Compson, comes to Jefferson in 1811 and, amassing money by clerking for an Indian trading agent, eventually purchases a fertile square mile in what will become the center of Jefferson.

From this classic plantation the Compsons launch political careers—the next generation producing a governor—but the succeeding generation already begins to decline. The grandfather of *The Sound and the Fury*'s Quentin fails as a military man in the Civil War, places the Compson plantation in mortgage during Reconstruction, and sires Jason III, the failed lawyer we know as Mr. Compson in *The Sound and the Fury*. The disarray of the current generation of Compsons appears against the southern background of personal hubris and chicanery in the midst of the violently discriminatory world of slaveholding—the very elements Quentin comes to hate in *Absalom*.

Moreover, the Compson Appendix confirms that such patterns of exploitation extend into the commodity and credit capitalism of the New South. As soon as Mrs. Compson dies in 1933, Jason sends Benjy to the state asylum and sells the house. He flourishes for a while as the owner of his own farmers' supply store and as a cotton trader. The appendix firmly accepts the newly impersonal society that has replaced the vestiges of the Old South. When Caddy's picture appears in a magazine, both Jason and Dilsey refuse to recognize her; the cult of nostalgia seems firmly dead by 1946, perhaps having already accomplished its work of preparing for the emergence of the New South two and more decades before. For all that, the narrator's tone in the Compson Appendix bestows a little more honor on the Compson line. Even Jason garners the tribute of being "the childless bachelor in whom ended that long line of men who had had something in them of decency and pride even after they had begun to fail at the integrity and the pride had become mostly vanity and selfpity" (NCE, 231).

Here Faulkner indulges himself, I would argue, in memorializing the racial strain embodied in the Compsons, that Presbyterian uprightness and firmness of will that somehow was betrayed by the material conditions of their southern opportunity. Though I cannot elaborate on this question, Faulkner's residual nostalgia here suggests one dimension of his attitude toward the persistent racial and economic woes of the South and anticipates his anguish over the final struggle toward desegregation in the 1950s. Faulkner's eventual realization that southern racism would have to be enjoined actively by white and black protest alike led him to write a series of public letters supporting peaceful, southern-controlled desegregation. This realization also prompted an important novel on the question, *Intruder in the Dust* (1948), in which a white teenager named Charles Mallison, highly reminiscent of Quentin Compson, works to exonerate a black man falsely accused of murdering a white man. In language often deliberately suggestive of *The Sound and the Fury*, Mallison accepts the necessity of rejecting the racist paternalism that constitutes the legacy of his family and his town.

Bibliography

Primary

Novels

The Sound and the Fury: The Corrected Text. New York: Random House, 1984; Vintage paperback, 1987.

As I Lay Dying: The Corrected Text. New York: Vintage paperback, 1987.

Absalom, Absalom!: The Corrected Text. New York: Random House, 1986; Vintage paperback, 1987.

Critical Editions

The Sound and the Fury. Edited by David Minter. Norton Critical Edition. New York: W. W. Norton, 1987. Reprint of the corrected text; supplemental material includes Faulkner's remarks on the novel, the Compson Appendix (which no longer appears in the 1987 corrected Vintage edition), and excerpts from selected criticism. *William Faulkner Manuscripts 6.* Edited by Noel Polk. Vols. 1 and 2: *The Sound and the Fury.* Holograph manuscript and miscellaneous pages; typescript. New York: Garland, 1987. Facsimile of Faulkner's working drafts of the novel.

Short Fiction

The Collected Stories. New York: Random House, 1950. (Includes "That Evening Sun," "Justice.")

Uncollected Stories. New York: Random House, 1979. (Includes "Lion.")

Letters, Interviews, Essays, and Speeches

Essays, Speeches, and Public Letters. Edited by James B. Meriwether. New York: Random House, 1965.

The Faulkner-Cowley File: Letters and Memories, 1944–62. Edited by Malcolm Cowley. New York: Viking, 1966.

Faulkner in the University: Class Conferences at the University of Virginia, 1957–1958. Edited by Frederick L. Gwynn and Joseph L. Blotner. New York: Random House, 1965.

"An Introduction for *The Sound and the Fury.*" Edited by James B. Meriwether. *Southern Review* 8 (October 1972):705–10. *Mississippi Quarterly* 26 (Summer 1973):410–15. Reprinted in Norton Critical Edition, 218–24.

Lion in the Garden: Interviews with William Faulkner, 1926–1962. Edited by James B. Meriwether and Michael Millgate. New York: Random House, 1968.

William Faulkner: Selected Letters. Edited by Joseph Blotner, New York: Random House, 1977.

Secondary

Biography

Blotner, Joseph. *Faulkner: A Biography.* 2 vols. New York: Random House, 1974.

———. *Faulkner: A Biography.* New York: Random House, 1984. A shortened version of the two-volume biography, it also includes some new material. Better for beginning students of Faulkner.

Gresset, Michel. *A Faulkner Chronology,* translated by Arthur B. Scharff. Jackson: University of Mississippi Press, 1985. Summary of important events in Faulkner's life and background.

Minter, David. *William Faulkner: His Life and Work.* Baltimore: Johns Hopkins University Press, 1980. Examines relation between Faulkner's life and his fiction.

Bibliography

Bassett, John Earl. *William Faulkner: An Annotated Checklist of Criticism.* New York: David Lewis, 1972.

———. *Faulkner: An Annotated Checklist of Recent Criticism.* N.p.: Kent State University Press, 1983.

McHaney, Thomas L. *William Faulkner: A Reference Guide.* Boston: G.K. Hall, 1976.

Criticism on Faulkner

Books

Bassett, John Earl, ed., *William Faulkner: The Critical Heritage.* London: Methuen, 1975.

Bleikasten, André. *The Most Splendid Failure: Faulkner's "The Sound and the Fury."* Bloomington: Indiana University Press, 1976. Formalist and psychological reading of the novel.

———, ed. *The Sound and the Fury: A Casebook.* New York: Garland, 1982. Background documents and selection of critical articles.

Brodhead, Richard, ed. *Faulkner: New Perspectives.* Englewood Cliffs, N.J.: Prentice-Hall, 1983. Collection of recent essays on Faulkner.

Brooks, Cleanth. *William Faulkner: The Yoknapatawpha Country.* New Haven, Conn.: Yale University Press, 1963. Chapter devoted to time, religion, and lost ideals in the novel.

Cohn, Dorrit. *Transparent Minds: Narrative Modes for Presenting Consciousness in Fiction.* Princeton, N.J.: Princeton University Press, 1978. Section on monologue stream-of-consciousness in the novel.

Cowan, Michael H., ed. *Twentieth Century Interpretations of "The Sound and the Fury."* Englewood Cliffs, N.J.: Prentice-Hall, 1968. Collection of important early articles on the novel, including selected remarks by Faulkner on the novel and Evelyn Scott's prepublication essay.)

Davis, Thadious. *Faulkner's "Negro": Art and the Southern Context.* Baton Rouge: Louisiana State University Press, 1983. Study of Faulkner's conception of blacks; chapter on the novel emphasizes the role of the Gibson family.

Hoffman, Frederick J., and Olga Vickery, ed. *William Faulkner: Two Decades of Criticism.* East Lansing: University of Michigan Press, 1951. Collection of important essays on Faulkner.

————. *William Faulkner: Three Decades of Criticism.* East Lansing: University of Michigan Press, 1960.

Hönnighausen, Lothar. *William Faulkner: The Art of Stylization in His Early Graphic and Literary Work.* Cambridge: Cambridge University Press, 1987. Faulkner's relations to popular art movements in his formative period.

Howe, Irving. *William Faulkner: A Critical Study.* 3d ed. Chicago: University of Chicago Press, 1975. Chapters on the major novels concentrating on social issues such as race and class.

Irwin, John T. *Doubling & Incest/Repetition & Revenge.* Baltimore: Johns Hopkins University Press, 1975. Psychoanalytic reading of the Compsons, especially Quentin, both in *The Sound and the Fury* and *Absalom, Absalom!*.

Kartiganer, Donald M. *The Fragile Thread: The Meaning of Form in Faulkner's Fiction.* Amherst: University of Massachusetts Press, 1979. Analysis of fragmentary form and modernist aesthetics; chapter on the novel.

Kinney, Arthur F. *Faulkner's Narrative Poetics: Style as Vision.* Amherst: University of Massachusetts Press, 1978. Reader's role in constructing meaning out of Faulkner's deliberately ambiguous texts.

————, ed. *Critical Essays on William Faulkner: The Compson Family.* Boston: G.K. Hall, 1982. Reprints related apprentice pieces. Selected reviews and criticism of the novel.

Kreiswirth, Martin. *William Faulkner: The Making of a Novelist.* Athens: University of Georgia Press, 1983. Background in Faulkner's earlier writing, especially his poetry, for the novel.

Matthews, John T. *The Play of Faulkner's Language.* Ithaca, N.Y.: Cornell University Press, 1982. Study of Faulkner's conception of language in fiction. Chapter on the novel studies the relation of expression and loss.

Millgate, Michael. *The Achievement of William Faulkner.* New York: Random House, 1966. Accounts of composition; critical readings of all the novels, with a chapter on each.

Porter, Carolyn. *Seeing and Being: The Plight of the Participant Observer in Emerson, James, Adams, and Faulkner.* Middletown, Conn.: Wesleyan University Press, 1981. Study of Faulkner's attitudes toward the South; influence of historical themes on aesthetics.

Sensibar, Judith. *The Origins of Faulkner's Art.* Austin: University of Texas Press, 1984. Identifies influences on Faulkner's poetry and early fiction.

Slatoff, Walter. *Quest for Failure: A Study of William Faulkner.* Ithaca, N.Y.: Cornell University Press, 1960. Study of Faulkner's style of paradox and inconclusiveness.

Stonum, Gary Lee. *Faulkner's Career: An Internal Literary History.* Ithaca,

N.Y.: Cornell University Press, 1979. Account of Faulkner's development of aesthetic technique; *The Sound and the Fury* as a turning point.

Sundquist, Eric J. *Faulkner: The House Divided.* Baltimore: Johns Hopkins University Press, 1983. Faulkner's struggle with the issue of race in his fiction; chapter on repression of race in the novel.

Swiggart, Peter. *The Art of Faulkner's Novels.* Austin: University of Texas Press, 1962. Chapter on time and morality in the novel.

Vickery, Olga W. *The Novels of William Faulkner.* Baton Rouge: Louisiana State University Press, 1959. Chapter on Compson brothers' differences; formal unities of the novel.

Volpe, Edmond L. *A Reader's Guide to William Faulkner.* New York: Farrar, Straus, 1964. Sound introduction to the novels; chronologies.

Wadlington, Warwick. *Reading Faulknerian Tragedy.* Ithaca, N.Y.: Cornell University Press, 1987. Performance of ritual and the recognition of tragedy in southern culture; chapter on the novel.

Wagner, Linda W., ed. *Faulkner: Four Decades of Criticism.* East Lansing: University of Michigan Press, 1973.

Warren, Robert Penn, ed. *Faulkner: A Collection of Critical Essays. Twentieth Century Views.* Englewood Cliffs, N.J.: Prentice-Hall, 1966.

Wittenberg, Judith Bryant. *Faulkner: The Transfiguration of Biography.* Lincoln: University of Nebraska Press, 1979. Faulkner's fiction as a transformation of crucial events in his life.

Wyatt, David M. *Prodigal Son: A Study in Authorship and Authority.* Baltimore: Johns Hopkins University Press, 1979. Chapter on the pattern of Faulkner's rebellion against an eventual acceptance of family and regional legacies.

Articles

Many of the most informative critical essays on the novel, as well as many of Faulkner's most revealing remarks about it (such as the drafts for his intended introduction) have been reprinted in the collections listed above. Brodhead's *New Perspectives*, Bleikasten's *Casebook*, and Minter's Norton Critical Edition all have fuller bibliographies listing work on *The Sound and the Fury*. I have listed a few important articles below that have not been reprinted, or are too recent to appear in the latest bibliographies, or to which I refer specifically in my reading above.

Aiken, Conrad. "William Faulkner: The Novel as Form." *Atlantic Monthly* 164 (November 1939): 650–54. Reprinted in *Twentieth Century Views*, 46–52.

Aswell, Duncan. "The Recollection and the Blood: Jason's Role in *The Sound and the Fury*." *Mississippi Quarterly* 21 (Summer 1968): 211–18. Reprinted in *Casebook*. Jason's relation to other brothers' concerns.

Beck, Warren. "William Faulkner's Style." *American Prefaces* 6 (Spring 1941): 195–211. Reprinted in *Twentieth Century Views*, 53–65.

Cecil, L. Moffitt. "A Rhetoric for Benjy." *Southern Literary Journal* 3 (Fall 1970):32–46. Reprinted in *Casebook*.

Coindreau, Maurice-Edgar. "Preface to *The Sound and the Fury*," translated by George M. Reeves. *Mississippi Quarterly* 19 (Summer 1966):107–15. Excerpted in Cowan.

Collins, Carvel. "The Pairing of *The Sound and the Fury* and *As I Lay Dying*." *Princeton University Library Chronicle* 18 (Spring 1957):115–19.

———. "The Interior Monologues of *The Sound and the Fury*." In *English Institute Essays 1952*, edited by Alan S. Downer, 29–56. New York: Columbia University Press, 1954.

Ellison, Ralph. "Twentieth-Century Fiction and the Black Mask of Humanity." In *Shadow and Act*, 24–44. New York: Random House, 1953; Vintage, 1964. Distortion of black characters in fiction by whites, including the earlier Faulkner.

Iser, Wolfgang. "Perception, Temporality, and Action as Modes of Subjectivity. William Faulkner: *The Sound and the Fury*." In *The Implied Reader: Patterns of Communication in Prose Fiction from Bunyan to Beckett*, 136–52. Baltimore: Johns Hopkins University Press, 1974. Reader's role in filling in the absent center of the novel with meaning. Reader response criticism.

Kartiganer, Donald M. "*The Sound and the Fury* and Faulkner's Quest for Form." *ELH* 37 (December 1970):613–39.

Lowrey, Perrin H. "Concepts of Time in *The Sound and the Fury*." In *English Institute Essays 1952*. edited by Alan S. Downer, 57–82. New York: Columbia University Press, 1954.

Mellard, James M. "Faulkner's Jason and the Tradition of Oral Narrative." *Journal of Popular Culture* 2 (Fall 1968): 195–210.

Meriwether, James B. "Notes on the Textual History of *The Sound and the Fury*." *The Papers of the Bibliographical Society of America* 56 (1962):285–316. Comprehensive history of the composition of the novel.

Morrison, Gail M. "The Composition of *The Sound and the Fury*." Original publication in *Casebook*, 33–64.

O'Donnell, George Marion. "Faulkner's Mythology." *Kenyon Review* 1 (Summer 1939):285–99.

Pitavy, François. "Through the Poet's Eye: A View of Quentin Compson." Original publication in *Casebook*, 79–100.

Bibliography

Ross, Stephen M. "The 'Loud World' of Quentin Compson." *Studies in the Novel* 7 (Summer 1975):245–57. Quentin's horror of talk and voices.

Samway, Patrick. "June 2, 1910: An Historic Day." In *Faulkner and History,* edited by Javier Coy and Michel Gresset, 111–36. Salamanca, Spain: Ediciones Universidad de Salamanca, 1986.

Sartre, Jean-Paul. "On *The Sound and the Fury:* Time in the Work of Faulkner." In *Literary and Philosophical Essays,* translated by Annette Michelson, 79–87. London: Rider & Co., 1955. Reprinted in Norton Critical Edition, 253–59.

Scott, Evelyn. "On William Faulkner's *The Sound and the Fury.*" New York: Cape & Smith, 1929.

S[mith], H[enry Nash]. "Three Southern Novels." *Southwest Review* 15 (Autumn 1929): iii–iv.

Weinstein, Philip M. "Meditations on the Other: Faulkner's Rendering of Women." In *Faulkner and Women: Faulkner and Yoknapatawpha, 1985,* edited by Doreen Fowler and Ann J. Abadie, 81–99. Jackson: University of Mississippi Press, Faulkner's distanced representation of women characters.

———. "'If I Could Say Mother': Construing the Unsayable About Faulknerian Maternity." In *Faulkner's Discourse,* edited by Lothar Hönnighausen, 3–16. Tübingen: Neimeyer: 1989. Study of maternity in *The Sound and the Fury,* concentrating on Caroline Compson.

Background

Cash, W. J. *The Mind of the South.* New York: Knopf, 1941; Vintage, 1960.

Dekker, George. *The American Historical Romance.* Cambridge: Cambridge University Press, 1987.

Fiedler, Leslie. *Love and Death in the American Novel.* New York: Dell Publishing Co.; new revised edition, 1969.

Genovese, Eugene D. *Roll, Jordan, Roll: The World the Slaves Made.* New York: Random House, 1972.

Gray, Richard J. *The Literature of Memory: Modern Writers of the American South.* Baltimore: Johns Hopkins University Press, 1976. Southern literary tradition; a chapter on Faulkner.

King, Richard H. *A Southern Renaissance: The Cultural Awakening of the American South, 1930–1955.* New York: Oxford University Press, 1980. Cultural background of period in the South; section on Faulkner.

Seidel, Kathryn Lee. *The Southern Belle in the American Novel.* Gainesville: University Presses of Florida, 1985.

Thoreau, Henry David. *Walden and Civil Disobedience,* edited by Owen Thomas. New York: W. W. Norton, 1966.

Tindall, George B. *The Emergence of the New South, 1913–1946.* Baton Rouge: Louisiana State University Press, 1967.

Woodward, C. Vann. *Origins of the New South, 1877–1913.* Baton Rouge: Louisiana State University Press, 1951; updated edition, 1971.

Index

The Author

John T. Matthews is the author of *The Play of Faulkner's Language* and a number of essays and reviews about Faulkner. He is currently the editor of *The Faulkner Journal*. His publications include criticism on other novelists as well, among them Emily Brontë, John Updike, and John Barth. He has held a fellowship from the National Endowment for the Humanities and serves on the editorial boards of *Arizona Quarterly* and *University of Mississippi Studies in English*. He teaches at Boston University.